Dearest Jna
Our stories unify

Beyond Lumpia, Pansit, and Seven Manangs Wild

Stories from the Heart of Filipino Americans

Mabuhay
Vangie Canonizado Buell

Beyond Lumpia, Pansit, and Seven Manangs Wild

Stories from the Heart of Filipino Americans

Edited by
Evangeline Canonizado Buell
Edwin Lozada
Eleanor Hipol Luis
Evelyn Luluquisen
Tony Robles
Myrna Ziálcita

A project of Filipino American National Historical Society, East Bay Chapter

Eastwind Books of Berkeley
Berkeley, California

First Edition
Copyright © 2014 by Filipino American National Historical Society, East Bay Chapter
All rights reserved

*No part of this publication may be reproduced or transmitted
by any form or by any means without prior permission of the editors.*

Editors: Evangeline Canonizado Buell, Edwin Lozada, Eleanor Hipol Luis
Evelyn Luluquisen, Tony Robles, Myrna Zialcita

Cover Art: Lewis Suzuki
Cover and Text Design: Edwin Lozada

ISBN: 978-0-692-02154-5
LCCN: 2014939966
This books was made possible by Eastwind Books of Berkeley
and a grant from City of Berkeley Arts Commission

Acknowledgments of previously published works:
"Babaylan in Playland By the Sea" by Oscar Peñaranda, published in *Tayo Literary Magazine*,
Issue 4, December 22, 2013; "The Two USAs" by O. Peñaranda, published in *Poor Magazine*

"Blackapina, Third Movement: The Blend," from *Midnight Peaches, Two O'clock Patience*,
J. Stickmon (Broken Shackle Publishing, 2012)

"Hey, Brown Man" by Juanita Tamayo Lott appeared in *Third World Women*
edited by Janice Mirikitani (Glide Foundation, San Francisco, CA, 1972)

"Human Removal" by Juanita Tamayo Lott, Copyright 1976, Juanita Tamayo Lott,
appeared in *Summary and Recommendations: Conference on Pacific/Asian American Families
and HEW Related Issues* (US Department of Health, Education and Welfare, May, 1978)

"My Life as a Lumpia" by Jessica Jamero, published in *Talk Story*, Filipino American National
History Society, Central Valley Chapter (Carpenter Printing, Merced, CA, 2008)

Portions of "If I Were a King" by Carlos Zialcita, published in the January 15, 2013 issue of
Positively Filipino magazine: "Joe Bataan: Ordinary Guy With An Extraordinary Heart"
Lyrics from "If I Were A King" by Joe Bataan is used with permission from the artist.

"My Gay Father and the Supreme Court" by Nikki Vilas appeared in *Positively Filipino* magazine, April 2013.

Published by
Eastwind Books of Berkeley
2066 University Avenue
Berkeley, California, 94704
EMAIL: eastwindbooks@gmail.com
http://www.asiabookcenter.com

Printed in the United States of America

ACKNOWLEDGMENTS

Maraming Salamat
EVANGELINE CANONIZADO BUELL

Many thanks to the family, the clan, and the village for their support:

Eastwind Books of Berkeley, Publisher
FANHS East Bay Chapter Executive Board
    Vicky Santos, President
    Renato Alfonso, Vice President
    Myrna Ziálcita, Secretary
    Evangeline Canonizado Buell, Treasurer and President Emerita FANHS
    Evelyn Luluquisen, Treasurer
Tom Bates, Mayor of The City of Berkeley
Bill Buell
Piedmont Gardens
Manilatown Heritage Foundation

To the Editorial Board: Evangeline Canonizado Buell, Evelyn Luluquisen, Eleanor Hipol Luis, Edwin Lozada, Tony Robles, and Myrna Ziálcita

To The Artists: Lewis Suzuki, Illustrator; Edwin Lozada, Layout

We commend Jeanette Lazam for helping to make this book possible as one of the former editors.

We give special thanks to Erika Pallasigue for her contribution.

Our special thanks to the City of Berkeley Arts Commission. Their two-year support of this project made completion of this book possible.

DEDICATION TO HELEN C. TORIBIO
Evangeline Canonizado Buell

*W*e honor Helen Cabulejo Toribio, the late editor of the FANHS Anthology of Filipino American Writers, *Seven Card Stud with 7 Manangs Wild*. Helen was a professor of Filipino American History at San Francisco State University and City College of San Francisco, a community activist, and a leader.

Helen, one of the founders of the Filipino American National Historical Society-East Bay, was truly the majestic flower in the FANHS Literary Garden. She caressed and inspired the writers to bloom and flower with prose and poetry. She left us a great and important legacy and was a beacon of light to the new budding Filipino American writers.

Helen's inspiration continues to encourage us and many of her students to continue writing and documenting our stories, the Filipino American experiences, because if "we do not tell our own story, then others will tell it for us, as they interpret it, and we will risk losing the essence and truth about the Filipino American experience. That history could fade from memory and one day our children's children could be asking, Who were our ancestors? What were they like? What did they do?" And there could be no one to answer and nowhere to look. I quote Helen Toribio, "May we have many more stories to write and share."

DEDICATION TO BILL SORRO AND AL ROBLES
Tony Robles

*B*ill Sorro and Al Robles, sons of Manilatown, sons of the *manongs* and sons of the I-Hotel. Bill and Al, whose poems are written in *lechon* skin, whose lives are danced in barrio fiesta songs, whose feet moved across the carabao mud of the I-Hotel, collecting the stories and songs and tears of the first generation of *manongs* and *manangs* in this country. They looked into the eyes of the *manongs* and *manangs* and saw life clearly, as a salmon sees, as it travels its way home, cutting across the water of memory. Bill and Al, whose dedication to the community and our stories and our art and our youth and elders were always with us—and still are. It was Al who said,

> *ako ay Pilipino—from across the 7000 islands & seas*
> *i am the blood-earth patis flowing thru the mountain*
> *soil-veins of my people*

And Bill Sorro who said, "We were trying to change the world, and quite frankly, you know, most of us still are. We still feel the same wonderful anger towards the system. And I really feel that it is important, particularly for young people, to be pissed off but to channel it, channel it with your love."

We dedicate this book, this work of love to you Bill Sorro and Al Robles, whose love for food and music and poetry and unending dedication and love for the Filipino community gave us the best of our community. As Al once wrote,

> *Our struggle is the best*
> *Part of our poetry*
> *And our poetry is the best*
> *Part of our struggle*

Bill Sorro and Al Robles, *presente*!

TRIBUTE TO FRED CORDOVA
Evangeline Canonizado Buell

We pay tribute to Fred Cordova, founder and leader of the Filipino American National Historical Society, also responsible for why the United States celebrates October as Filipino American History Month.

This book could not have been possible if it had not been for him and his wife, Dorothy Laigo Cordova, who paved the way for Filipinos in America to document our history. Both Dorothy and Fred, Filipino American historians, established this prestigious community-based organization on November 26, 1982 "to promote understanding, education, enlightenment, appreciation, and enrichment through gathering, identification, preservation, and dissemination of the history and culture of Filipino Americans in the United States."

Fred headed and maintained the archives at the headquarters of FANHS National in Seattle, Washington. He was the inspiration and mentor in helping Filipino Americans to be proud to be Filipino, and proud of our culture, history, and heritage. Fred led us in ethnic spirit and solidarity. He enriched the lives of Filipinos in America, Filipinos all over the world, and the community at large. He is a Filipino American historical gem.

We quote Fred Cordova:

> "Everybody doesn't have to be a hero; everybody doesn't have to be famous. Each person who's Filipino American, to me, is very, very important as a story. Our stories are really in our people. It's not so much in what the achievements are...as much as what is the story itself."

Fred Cordova
(1931 – 2013)
www.fanhs-national.org

Contents

Introduction ... 1

Identity and Assimilation

Renelaine Bontol-Pfister	• *Ginger Sleeping*	5
Titania Buchholdt	• *On My Birth Certificate*	9
Ann Fajilan	• *Ann*	13
Wilfred Galila	• *Perhaps the Coyote Knows*	17
Juanita Tamayo Lott	• *Hey, Brown Man*	22
Eleanor Hipol Luis	• *Finding the NOLA Root*	23
Elea Luis Manalo	• *Hindi Ako Nakakaintindi*	26
Tony Robles	• *Whisper, Carabao*	30
Jeanine Silverio	• *A Visit to Grandpa's House*	34
Adrian James Sobredo	• *Filipino American Identity: A Teenager's Experience*	38
Janet Stickmon	• *Blackapina— Third Movement: The Blend*	45
Clifton Trinidad	• *I Am an American*	50
Nikki Vilas	• *My Gay Father and the Supreme Court*	54
Carlos Ziálcita	• *If I Were a King*	59

Cultural Bridges

Jeffrey Tangonan Acido	• *Letter To My Kadkadua*	67
Jeannie Barroga	• *Haunted*	71
Evangeline Canonizado Buell	• *Tribute to Oscar*	75
Tess Crescini	• *Birth to the Ancient in New Time*	77
Brenda Manuel Fulton	• *Dominador Cruz Manuel*	79
	• *Filipino Weddings*	84
Herb Jamero	• *The Raid*	88
Jessica A. Jamero	• *My Life as a Lumpia*	93
Emily Porcincula Lawsin	• *Papa's Two Left Feet*	97
Jeanette Gandionco Lazam	• *Aunties Win Tram Ride at Hanauma Bay*	102

Cultural Bridges

Juanita Tamayo Lott	• *Uncle Paul Lives on Minna Street in Central City*	104
Evelyn Luluquisen	• *Attitude Adjustment*	106
Rebecca Mabanglo-Mayor	• *Gift of Plums*	110
Lisa Suguitan Melnick	• *Agtawid (Inheritance)*	115
	• *Out the Back Door*	119
Veronica Montes	• *Beauty Queens*	123
Oscar Peñaranda	• *Babaylan in Playland by the Sea*	128
Felicia Perez	• *Initiation: My Filipino Tattoo Experience*	136
Robert V. Ragsac, Sr.	• *Sakada*	140
Marivic Reyes-Restivo	• *Nana Meng's Tsokolate*	145
Tony Robles	• *Up and Down*	149
Michele Santos-Gutierrez	• *Stirred*	153
Lourdes Sobredo	• *Snippets of Grandpa's Simple Life in America*	158
Monica Valerio	• *A Life Forgotten*	163
Jean Vengua	• *The Social Box*	167

Discrimination and Struggle

Kayla Crow	• *Love Letter for the Women of the World*	177
Mel Vera Cruz	• *In Transit*	180
Brenda Manuel Fulton	• *The First Grade*	182
Jeanette Gandionco Lazam	• *Walls and a Place Called Manila Town*	184
Gwen Florelei Luib	• *Chalk Dust*	188
Oscar Peñaranda	• *The Two USAs*	193
Victoria Santos	• *A Questionable Legacy*	195
Juanita Tamayo Lott	• *Human Removal*	200
Justine Villanueva	• *Educating Justine*	202
Peter Kenichi Yamamoto	• *Beef Stew, Maybe Tripe*	206

Biographies	213
Glossary	223

INTRODUCTION

*B*eyond *Lumpia, Pansit, and Seven Manangs Wild* features many stories about our second, third, and fourth generation Filipinos, their experiences on how they identify or not as Filipinos in America. The narratives reflect the nature of living influenced by multiple cultures and some reveal the pride felt by the authors in their Filipino heritage through their stories and poetry, as in Tess Crescini's "Birth of the Ancient in New Times." Many Filipino Americans in the U.S. maintain strong bonds with family and friends in the Philippines. For some, their parents and grandparents serve as the sole bridge to the islands. There are also those who still cling to the Philippine culture, but have a strong allegiance to the U.S., especially the older second generation (70s to 80s) who may visit the islands but not return to live.

Food is an integral part of the culture. In "My Life as a Lumpia," Jessica Jamero tells how the simple act of rolling *lumpia* awakens cultural pride. Pete Yamamoto's poem, "Beef Stew, Maybe Tripe," shows how the Filipino culture of food unites us. Instead of always giving in to American hamburgers and hot dogs, the act of longing and savoring *adobo, lumpia,* and *pansit* helps us resist complete assimilation and through our senses helps us retain elements of our unique identity. Through our writing, we combat amnesia and what destiny would otherwise hold for us, the casting of our personal stories and histories to oblivion.

EDITORS
Evangeline Canonizado Buell, Eleanor Hipol Luis, Edwin Lozada,
Evelyn Luluquisen, Tony Robles, Myrna Ziálcita

Identity and Assimilation

GINGER SLEEPING

Renelaine Bontol-Pfister

Melanie opened her eyes, but she didn't want to get out of bed. What was there to do today? Since being out of a job four weeks ago, she had cleaned their entire house, including brushing away the cobwebs collecting at the corners of the ceilings. She had scrubbed the toilets clean. She had vacuumed the carpet and bleached the bath tubs. She had dusted every piece of furniture, every lamp and tiny decoration in the house.

Well, there was always Ginger, the pit bull/retriever mix they'd rescued from the shelter a couple of months ago. Ginger needed her.

But first she stayed in bed and prayed the Rosary, like she had in the last eighteen months. She had promised to pray the Rosary until she and her husband, Carl, received their green cards. Her mother had told her to keep doing it because Mama Mary was going to intercede for her.

Melanie wasn't sure she believed it, after waiting not just the last year and a half, but really the last seven years for the green card. She was an occupational therapist, and was first sponsored by an employer in New York for an EB3 visa. Almost five years passed before Melanie and Carl decided to move to the West Coast. Another employer had promised to file for an EB2 visa for them, which was processed much faster than the EB3. Usually it took less than a year. Now it has been eighteen months.

And Melanie cannot work. Her employment authorization card had expired a month ago, and she was waiting for the new one. Although she had called Immigration to follow up on both the EAD and the EB2 visa, all the answers she'd received were "you have to wait fifteen days for a response," "you have to wait twenty-one days for a response." They've gone to the local USCIS office and filed service requests. They've written letters and emails. The last letter she'd received from USCIS stated that her petition was an EB3, not an EB2. She photocopied her documents clearly reflecting the EB2 petition and enclosed a letter and sent it all to USCIS.

All she can do now is wait.

That was the hardest task. Waiting with no knowledge of what could happen. What was she going to do if she still couldn't work? Her savings were dwindling. In another month she didn't know how she was going to pay for the rent, water, electricity, cable, cell phone, credit card bills, car insurance and car payments.

And the worst thought was: what if they got denied the visa altogether? What would they do? Where would they go?

Melanie's head hurt from all the obsessing. And the itchy area on the right side of her torso had progressively become redder and larger the last few days. She got out of bed and examined herself in the bathroom mirror. She was distressed to see small boils forming on the red area. When she touched it, she felt as if someone had slit her skin with a blade.

She wanted to go the doctor, but she didn't have health insurance since she wasn't working.

She thought about her home in Cebu. Her parents lived there with their dozen dogs. Their house, close to the beach, was her mother's ancestral home. When her grandparents were still alive and lived there, she and her cousins spent summer vacations there—running in the yard, sliding down the ramp using large banana leaves, playing hide and seek in the dark rooms, and swimming in the ocean for entire days.

She missed the life in the Philippines. It never got as lonely as it was in America, because there was always someone stopping by the house, whether it was her parents' friends or vendors selling *kutsinta* or *banana cue*. It was easy to text her friends and meet them at the mall for a movie or to window shop.

In America there was no one. You can't stop by your neighbor's house unannounced; you had to call and schedule first. Melanie's friends were working and had children; she didn't want to bother them.

So there was nothing to do but clean and cook and watch TV. And wait.

Sometimes she wondered if it would be better to just give up. Grab a knife from the kitchen and bleed herself dry. Make the agonizing frustration go away. But she'd see their dog out in the yard, lying on her bed, sleeping under the heat of the sun. She liked to watch Ginger sleep. Her little legs twitched and sometimes she opened an eye in response to a strange noise, then she'd go back to sleep. It always made Melanie smile.

Melanie got a call from Carl as she parked the car at Costco. She wanted to buy some chicken breasts to cook for dinner.

"Check USCIS. They just approved your EAD. They're producing your card now."

She couldn't believe it.

It was one hurdle conquered, and for that she was grateful. At least now she could go back to work and pay the bills as they waited for the final hurdle: the green card.

On her way home, she stopped three cars down from the traffic light. She saw an older man wearing a checkered flannel shirt standing at the corner. He was holding up a homemade sign that said "Homeless vet. Please spare $1." It was a common sight in her area.

Since receiving the news about the EAD, she felt impelled to give this man something. She reached into her bag and retrieved a five-dollar bill from her wallet. She waved the bill so he could see she wanted to give it to him. He jogged the few steps over.

"Good luck to you. I know how it is. I've been out of a job myself," she said.

He took the money and looked at it. "Wow, thanks."

He looked so happy.

"I applied for disability and unemployment a month ago..." he started saying, but then the light changed to green and she had to go.

"Good luck!" she said again before driving away.

She thought about the way he looked when he saw the five-dollar bill, and she cried.

ON MY BIRTH CERTIFICATE

Titania Buchholdt

I was five years old when my mother showed me my birth certificate. After going over the layout of the form and reading all the entries with me, she left me to sit at the dining room table so I could study the document in detail.

I was a scholar, a first-grader at Nightingale Elementary in Venice, California. My mother was a third-grade teacher at St. Mark's Elementary, a private school in Los Angeles, and with her tutoring I had a third-grade reading level. In addition to teaching me reading and math, she encouraged me to analyze what I was reading. My birth certificate brought up many questions.

My parents were listed as Caucasian and Malay, one born in California and the other in the Philippines. I did not understand this. Why was my mother Malay, and not Filipino? Why was my father Caucasian and not American? And why was my father from a state while my mother was simply from a country? Didn't the Philippines have states, too?

And so I learned that the Philippines had provinces. As did Canada. And there was really no difference between a province and a state. But why would a country choose to have provinces instead of states? The answer was the easiest of adult reasons: because that was just the way it was.

As to why there was no listing of the name of the province where my mother was from, while my father was required to identify the state of his birth, there were two reasons. The first, and most likely, was that the little box on the form was too small to contain that much information. Second, the U.S. government workers who processed this information probably knew nothing about the provinces of the Philippines, so that detail would be useless. I knew this because my father was a U.S. government worker, and he frequently talked about how government workers hardly knew anything about the world.

The bigger question, why my mother was listed as Malay and not Filipino, was a more complicated issue, an issue of classification. Malay and Caucasian were races. Filipino and American were nationalities. Nationalities had everything to do with political boundaries, which were man-made, and always changeable. That was not to say that the boundaries of the Philippines or the boundaries of California were going to change any time soon, but people of any race could be born anywhere and, once they were grown up, could choose to change their nationality.

And then I saw there was something very, very important missing on my birth certificate. My mother's race and my father's race were listed, but what about me? What was my race? Both? Was "both" a race?

My mother informed me that, because it was 1963, my race was "Other." On government forms, I would be instructed to check off only one box when it came to identifying my race, and the only reasonable choice was "Other." I was not just "Oriental," and I was not just "White." I was something else altogether, and the government was going to have to guess what that was. That would be very hard to do since I didn't know the answer myself. It would be decades before the category "Mixed Race" would be used on forms, or even in conversation.

Two years later, when I was seven years old, my family moved to Anchorage, Alaska. One of the benefits of being a U.S. government worker was the opportunity to transfer to a job opening anywhere in the country, and my parents decided to experience life in the Last Frontier. In Anchorage, I found that my race was an even more complicated matter.

From the beginning, my younger brother and I learned that the tourists who roamed the downtown streets would not stop taking photos of us. We were the cutest brown-skinned kids these strangers had ever seen. It did not matter that I called out "We're not Eskimo! We're Filipino!" because the tourists just wanted to bring home pictures of photogenic brown-skinned children. My mother told us that there must be no brown-skinned children where those people lived, or if there were, those people ignored them.

By our second week in Alaska, my mother told me to cover my face if I saw people taking my photo, but how would I be able to see where I was going? I didn't want to fall off the sidewalk or trip on a curb while I crossed the street. Worse, my mother told me to cover my face and also cover my little brother's face. Now, what kind of life was that, walking down the street in hiding? We decided that we would need to avoid the downtown streets. We stayed at home as much as possible that summer, until tourist season ended.

Growing up in Alaska, I was constantly pegged as Yupik Eskimo. Or Athapaskan Indian. Tlingit. Korean. Hawaiian. Never as part Filipino, much less part Ilocano or part Ibanag. I often gave up trying to set people straight. Like the downtown tourists, the locals would think what they wanted. My race became whatever people thought it ought to be.

Two years later, when I was nine years old, my father took another transfer as a government worker, and my family drove to Atlanta, Georgia. It was a very long road trip from Anchorage. And as we entered the southern U.S., it became a scary road trip. Martin Luther King, Jr. had already been murdered. We were traveling to places where it was not safe for people of different races to mix.

My mother had very dark skin. Even as a child in the Philippines, she had experienced prejudice and racism on account of the tribal heritage of her father. As we drove across Texas my parents took note of the murders of both black and white civil rights activists happening in the South. Snipers were shooting at cars that contained both white and black passengers on the freeway.

Titania Buchholdt

After a brief family discussion, my parents told me and my brothers their plan: while my father drove the car, and while us kids behaved ourselves in the back seat, my mother would bend over and rest her face on her knees. All across Mississippi. That way, it would look like my father was driving a car with little kids in the back seat. And once we were in Alabama, it would be getting dark out, so my mother could resume sitting up in the car. In the meantime, we would have to be extra careful about going into gas stations. We needed to try not to use the bathroom until we got through Mississippi. And it would be up to me to make sure that my brothers didn't start fussing, since Mom couldn't sit up to take care of us.

All across Mississippi, I looked out the window and prayed that my mother would not be hit by a stray or intentional bullet. I prayed that nobody would notice that my brothers and I were not really white. I slouched in the back seat so nobody could see me, either, and I moved only when I got a cramp from lying so still. I thought about how my mother was not even black, and how that didn't matter to ignorant murderous racists. So many people did not know or want to know that, soon, the majority of people on this planet would not be white. And I thought long and hard about the fact that, really, my mother was Malay. That's what it says on my birth certificate.

ANN

Ann Fajilan

Somewhere between a real American and a Filipina there is a hybrid creature known as an Asian American. I never quite understood that moniker, but apparently I am one of "those" creatures. At least that is how I am characterized and categorized and commodified by others. My real story doesn't really figure into the social equation unless I put it on the table. Whenever I have offered to testify, I have been patronized and told that "your story has already been told." When you don't look like the cover girl American model with blonde hair and blue eyes, or an African American Jezebel or the "exotic" Middle Eastern Indian belly dancer, you must be some kind of brown faced immigrant/foreigner...either Mexican or some kind of Chinese; traditionally categorized as OTHER.

Whenever I have to claim ethnicity I write down American Filipino. I was born on American soil, and yes, New Mexico is not Mexico, but is indeed one of the 50 American states. So technically I am an American. Adjectives usually come before the noun but in my case the Filipino in me was eradicated. Not because my parents were ashamed of their homeland, but the cultural pressure to assimilate was so severe that they really believed that if they raised their American-born children separately but equally from their naturalized island offspring, we would be full-fledged *Americanos*. Well, we turned out to be proficient in American social customs and superficially superior to our blood relatives from the islands; at least that is what I believed as a pimply, greasy-haired seventh-grader U.S. citizen living on a U.S. military compound in Quezon City, Philippines, and attending the exclusive International American School one hour away in the city of Makati. Yes. It was a dreadful one-and-a-half-hour bus trip through the crowded streets of Quezon City, through the densely packed Quiapo *palenque*, alongside the Pasig River with its overpowering smells of poverty, past the mansions and cardboard squatter's huts adjacent to the twelve foot, barbed wire, cement compound walls. I never realized how many compounds I was shuttled to and from. If you are rich in the Philippines your house is full of servants, maids, drivers, gardeners and errand boys and girls. But in most rich households the servants, maids, drivers, gardeners and errand boys and girls are not your blood relatives. Because my father was in the U.S.A. Army, we were rich. If you have any idea of the economics of the Philippines, you are either rich or poor—mostly poor. But to a pimply, greasy-haired seventh-grader U.S. citizen trying to fit in with the non-Filipino American teenagers on base, I found it very challenging to acknowledge our "waitstaff" as my blood relatives. It was difficult enough dealing with pubescent peer pressures, teenage hierarchies, and letting the "cool" crowd watch me treat my favorite Aunt as my maid.

    I only really began to understand my official "other"ness when I began to apply for college. Of course back in the seventies there were only three boxes that appeared on all of the college applications. It eventually evolved into more boxes as Affirmative Action and ethnic scholarships became available. Then everyone in high school found some drop of blood in their ancestral tree. College peers, professors and advisors continually pointed out that many of "us" were there to satisfy the quota. What they didn't realize was that although I may have gotten there as a "seat filler," I was going to be one of those who stayed. I continually tell my students of color that no matter how you got here, you are here now, and there is no reason to leave the room. Represent, represent, represent.

    I have been teaching in the academic bubble for over twenty-five years,

Ann Fajilan

functions, I am still made aware of my professional "other"ness when I enter a faculty reception, a lecture hall, a paper presentation, a conference room—I don't even have to scan the room; that is done for me. I do not enter a designated room by mistake, and yet that is always the feeling that emanates from the room—unless of course I am one of the guests of honor and my picture has been prestigiously mounted on the dais or the program, then it is a very different reception of sorts. Walk in my shoes for a moment when I am not the honored one, when I am just another colleague coming into the space...when the tribe does not recognize me, it isn't just a polite nod of the head, a courteous greeting of sorts, but a clear laser beam that pierces through my face to anyone else entering the room. I am pretty sure I am not invisible, but maybe I am the one in denial. Or it might be that my 5'1" stature makes it much easier for me to be overlooked. In any case, I am made aware of my "other"ness on so many levels and it is exhausting. So I do not dwell on that. I just continue to enter many, many rooms to absorb and observe. Two days ago I was at the Kennedy Center American College Theatre Festival in Sacramento, CA and as I entered the Faculty Hospitality Room, it was as if I was entering a monolithic kingdom; as per usual I was the anomaly. The key point is that I entered and although I tried to find a reason to leave the room, I stayed. Perhaps it was the fine selection of cheese and sweets that kept me there.

Since my profession is theatre, communication and reading tableaux are second nature to me. So I do not think I am being paranoid, just particularly observant. I try and teach my students to read the social situations so they [...])vide them with ap- [...] they can take. I try [...] d relationships, and [...] ; to their advantage. [...] ow to gently inform [...] f this is a dance and

EDITORS' NOTE

Bottom of page 14, missing line after "...for over twenty-five years, ..."

...and even to this day when I go to conventions, conferences, and professional ...

that as Shakespeare said: "All the world's a stage, and all the men and women merely players." It is a multi-layered challenge for many of our students of diversity as they begin to penetrate enclaves that they have not been previously invited to.

One of the words that is commonly used when speaking about multiculturalism and diversity is *tolerance*. In the last decade we have been trying to teach tolerance. Even I thought that was a progressive word until I looked it up. It is the capacity to endure continued subjection to something, especially a drug, transplant, antigen, or environmental conditions, without adverse reaction. I explain to my students how a host/tess feels when someone brings an "And 1" to their party. This "And 1" was not invited because this "And 1" is unknown to the tribe. This foreign "And 1" has the potential to shake things up and disrupt the group dynamic so the host/tess becomes fearful that it can only be a harsh, negative experience in store for his/her partygoers. The subtext becomes: "I will politely tolerate their existence for the next three hours because I know there is a finite time that I will be subjected to endure continued subjection." I try to teach my students that we should not settle for tolerance in our future, but we should advocate inclusivity. We should not gain access to the room/the playing field because we came in on the arm of an ally or as an afterthought, but that we should work towards getting a bona fide invitation to the party or perhaps we need to start host/tessing a new kind of party.

PERHAPS THE COYOTE KNOWS

Wilfred Galila

We caught the next train after an hour of missing the first one. A clear, blue, cloudless sky ran overhead as we left the Amtrak station at Richmond on our way to Yosemite National Park.

It was a 5-hour trip with a bus transfer in Merced to get to Curry Village where we were meeting up with friends. The train was comfortable and had a bar. Cindy and I started to party at two in the afternoon with some beer. Her dark blonde hair was tied up in a ponytail and her blue eyes were drowsy by the time we arrived in Merced, where the heat was triple in intensity and only went down a few notches on the bus ride to Yosemite. We arrived and spent the night in the hut of a friend who worked at the national park.

The next morning, I took a shower. It was the last time that I used a real bathroom for the majority of the trip. We camped out for a week in the High Sierra desert.

We would leave our campsite and head to the nearest town during the day to escape the intense heat. On the fifth day, on our way to town, we stopped the car and waited for a huge flock of sheep to cross the endless highway. I was admiring the stampede of dirty wool and dusty cloud when a black sheep emerged from the gray mass. It scrambled around and started to run in the opposite direction. A sheepdog intercepted and forced it to join the herd.

That afternoon, we stopped by a pub to sample the local brew. I had a pint of what tasted like sagebrush. It was like drinking the desert.

The beer's diuretic properties kicked in and I headed to the restroom. Finally a real restroom, I thought to myself. I peed away the desert in me, washed my hands, and saw my reflection in the mirror. It's been quite a while since I've looked into one. I saw that my dark, straight greasy hair needed some washing, my shirt soiled with fun memories, and my slightly darker than brown face tanned from the desert sun. Staring at my reflection, I remembered an identity that, for a while, I forgot about, an identity that I wore every moment of my life.

I came out of the restroom self-conscious. My sense of self retreated deep into my being. I became aware that I was the only Filipino in the group. I became aware of being different. The unique culture and certain values that are deeply ingrained in my psyche surfaced for me to see. I wondered about my Filipino identity—something that no one in the group, including myself and, most likely, the entire crowd in the pub, seemed to really understand or would even think about. No one seemed to mind, so I kept to myself and finished the rest of the aromatic brew with thoughts of what I am and what I'm supposed to be.

We spent some time hanging out in other parts of the High Sierras during our stay. I stood in the middle of a desert, just off the highway, looking at the immense space strewn with various rock formations, fragrant sagebrush, and enormous mountains in the distance. I thought to myself, how could we do this? What brought us to swap this great beauty for a misshapen consumerist culture? A culture in which I had to give up a big part of me to be in, was brought up to want it, and learned ways of how to lose myself in it.

A coyote walked by, tearing through an illusion of a huge phantom city with skyscrapers that I have imagined onto the landscape. The coyote stood still, about twenty feet away, looked at me long enough to recognize what I am, perhaps what I'm supposed to be, then moved on.

It was the first time I was regarded by a wild animal in the U.S., and it did not seem to question my presence and purpose on American soil. At least not like the way I did and perhaps other people do.

Later, I realized that it wasn't until I came to the United States that I really began to see and tried to understand my Filipino identity. Is it in the way that I look? Is it in the color of my skin? It is in many ways. Yet it is, simultaneously, just a part of the equation, for I am a mix of different races and ethnicities, like a majority of Filipinos, as a result of waves of colonization. I explored my identity in the food I ate. I gave up meat years ago, for other reasons including what I've mentioned, and dwindled my options down to vegetable *lumpia*, vegetable *pansit*, and vegetarian *adobo*. At least I still enjoyed all kinds of Filipino deserts. But overall it was never the same. (Since the writing of this piece, I started eating meat again.) I tried to find it in my name. I have a Germanic/Old English first name and a Hebrew-sounding family name. These are names I acquired at birth. I respond to them since they are names that I am used to, otherwise they have no resonance in reflecting my Filipino identity.

Perhaps it could be in the language. I hear the resonance of identity in Filipino language. I speak my native tongues of Hiligaynon and Tagalog just as well as I speak English. There is a certain flavor to the meaning of words when said in a particular language. There is something quite profound in hearing and speaking in a language that I first used to recognize my spirit —a Filipino spirit. It is like a spear that cuts through. The potency of spouting profanity in a language that you know by heart is proof of this: "Motherfucker!" is as effective when running after a train that you missed in San Francisco, as "*Putang ina!*" is when you are stuck for hours in immobile traffic in the middle of EDSA in Manila, as "*Yudiputa!*" (a corruption of *hijo de puta* *) is when traffic bottleneck forms at the corner of Iznart, Ledesma, and JM Basa streets in Iloilo City.

Language is the most powerful of human inventions in generating realities and creating cultures. I assimilated well to American life through my

---

**hijo de puta: (Sp.) son of a whore*

proficiency in the English language but not without its share of confusion. The reality of my Filipino identity clashed with American culture. For instance, the Filipino trait of functioning as a community goes against the American ideal of individualism. It has been a constant struggle to tune this dissonance into a harmonious whole. Not to mention that the use of native Filipino languages has been reduced to optional status as a sacrifice in the name of assimilation and as a convenient way of operation in a western and English-speaking society. I can think with a western mind but I feel that I am a Filipino. But what does that really mean?

It is very possible that one day this identity and cultural struggle faced by most, if not all, Filipinos as well as the members of various diasporas, brought about by rabid westernization, will be pacified into obscurity, concealed and replaced by an identity and culture that is global. This metamorphosis began when the first wave of colonizers arrived on Philippine shores, an ongoing process in which we, as witnesses and participants, anticipate its tragic culmination in the far future.

It took about 400 years of Spanish rule and oppression, about 50 years of American rule, whose influence continues to this day, and a sprinkling from neighboring Asian nations of various cultures and sensibilities that has seeped into the deep, porous, and welcoming psyche of the Filipino people that has transformed the native Aeta into a post-colonial being chock-full of cultural hybridity.

True is the notion that the Philippines is the very pot in Southeast Asia where it all melted. And this melting continues in one of, if not the biggest pot of all: the U.S. of A.

I can think with a western mind but I feel that I am a Filipino. This came to mind again about a year later when I was hiking on Mount Diablo. Next to the trail, on a hill covered with dry grass that contrasted with the blue cloudless sky, walked a coyote. For all I knew it was the same one that I saw in the

Wilfred Galila

High Sierras. It stood still, looked at me long enough to recognize what I am, perhaps what I'm supposed to be, then moved on.

HEY, BROWN MAN

Juanita Tamayo Lott

For my 1968-1969 TWLF/SFSU Brothers

      Hey, brown man
      With your slight bronze back turned to me,
      I see your body bend and shake
      Exhaustion of revolution
      Aching for relaxation
      We part

      Twilight falls
      And you fall
      Resting on her full white breasts
      While I play with her brother

      Following sunrise we meet to speak
      Of oppression, liberation, and of hope
      Your purple lips pout in bitterness
      Grope for words

      But rhetoric of rice terraces is lost in last night's sheets.

      Hey brown man
      Turn around
      Make love to me

                Published in the anthology, *Third World Women*, 1972

FINDING THE NOLA ROOT:
[NOLA: New Orleans, Louisiana]

Eleanor Hipol Luis

St. Malo in Lake Bourne, St. Bernard Parish
    among the brown mud and reeds
Pinoys jumped from slave ships to escape
    from the Spanish bound for America
1763 documents the first Pinoys to flee
    and hide in the swamplands

Brothers of the village—a Portuguese negro,
A white *maestro* interpreter speaking Spanish
    and a Malay dialect, baptized the men
    into the Catholic rite
But no masses are held by any priest
No outsider comes to the village in the middle of the marsh

A village where the 'Malays' from the Philippines
    hide from the outsiders
No taxation, no police, no one but themselves
To decide the punishment for an angered fisherman
To decide their destiny

Life was among reptiles, birds and insects,
    Swarms of a thousand mosquitos,
        Slithering tappanoes (worms with green heads)

Eleanor Hipol Luis

Fighting was with insects eating the wood posts of the houses
    sitting high on stilts, built by the people and for the people
Materials carried no less than three miles from forest to swampland
Where alligator maimed chickens walk on one foot, or one leg
Where fish is dinner for both man and animal

In the far distance, a Manila restaurant is hidden
    in the court of the oldest New Orleans quarter
Supported by Spanish West Indian sailors
The Spanish and English menu carries good food at a fair price
But might be closed by the time you get there

Gambling in the evening passes the time
A Cantor sings the numbers in a poetic style, much like
    Latin prayers of the Catholic faith
Somehow, this has a feel of gambling with religious overtones
    while feeding on raw fish seasoned with vinegar and oil

The crimson bayou, muddy and surrounded with tall reeds
No illness
No liquor
No women in the cold and desolate bayou

The fishermen and alligator hunters
    throw their nets into the marsh to gather crawdads, shrimp,
    and other small crustaceans
Sail their handmade *bankas* farther out into the lake for the bigger catch
Then return to the village, to wait for the next day to repeat
Yesterday

Eleanor Hipol Luis

As we searched for our NOLA root,
Directions this way and that
Brought us to where it was said we used to be
No one heard of our shrimp farms
No one heard of our shrimp farmers
    of our fishermen
    of our villages

Many
Katrinas
have moved us
away
from the bayou

NOTE: *In 2007 and 2008 I joined a group that went to New Orleans, Louisiana (NOLA) to rebuild homes damaged by Hurricane Katrina. After one of our work sessions, we set out on a quest to find the site of St. Malo where the Filipino community once lived amongst the bayous and swamplands. Along the way we stopped to ask people where we could find this site, but instead we found that no one knew of our community, of our shrimp farms or of our farmers. The people we stopped for directions sent us to a community where people "looked like us," which ended up being the Vietnamese community. There we came across a non-profit organization, Mary Queen of Vietnam, that was working on rebuilding the Vietnamese community after Katrina. We were told that we were probably about 1-2 hours away from the bayous where the Filipinos once had a thriving community. The sun was going down; it was almost the end of the day. We were so close.*

HINDI AKO NAKAKAINTINDI

Elea Luis Manalo

Who knew that not understanding Tagalog would have such an impact on my life? I am a third generation American-born Filipino. My maternal grandmother was born in Vallejo, California where her immediate family resided for a short period of time while her father was in the military. She moved to the Philippines as a young child to General Trias, Cavite where she spent most of her adolescence. It wasn't until she was married with children that she moved back to the U.S. where she had her youngest two children, one of whom is my mother.

My parents were born and raised in California. Although my mom doesn't speak Tagalog, she does understand. When she was a child her parents spoke Tagalog frequently so she did learn the language. My dad, on the other hand, understands very little. My paternal grandparents were from different parts of the Philippines and spoke different dialects—Visayan and Ilocano. They tried communicating in Tagalog, but according to my grandmother, my grandfather's Tagalog was terrible. So they ended up speaking mainly English at home.

I was born in San Francisco and raised in Daly City, California. The grammar school I attended had a diverse population. It wasn't until I was about 11 years old when a friend pointed out to me that my mom didn't have an accent. I didn't think much of it before this comment, but after that I started to notice that most of the parents of my friends had accents. Not just the Filipinos, but also the parents of my friends that were Hispanic and Chinese spoke with accents.

Elea Luis Manalo

When I attended family parties with my friends, their family members all spoke with accents. While all of my family were so...Americanized.

While I was growing up, when I would hang out at the homes and parties of my Filipino friends, I was bombarded with questions like, "Why don't you understand Tagalog?" "Why didn't your parents teach you Tagalog?" And comments like, "I made sure my kids learned Tagalog." There were times I felt like I was being patronized for something I didn't have control over.

Through the years I came across more and more Filipinos in public places, like stores and churches, asking if I was Filipino. They almost always followed with the second question, "Do you understand Tagalog?" It became routine for me to beat them to the second question with an explanation—"Yes, I'm Filipino, but I do not understand Tagalog. My parents were born and raised in America." Sometimes they wouldn't ask if I understood Tagalog. They just assumed I did and started speaking to me. I would have to interrupt and give my explanation. I received one of two reactions to my explanation—one of acceptance or one that made me feel a bit guilty. I remember one day, I was having a dress hemmed by a Filipino seamstress when another customer walked in. They started conversing in Tagalog. They were laughing and talking and after the customer left, the seamstress continued to talk to me in Tagalog. I assumed she was letting me in on their conversation. I let her finish her story then told her that I did not understand what she was saying. Instead of translating, she just shook her head and said that it's a shame I couldn't understand. Of course I left there feeling down and out.

It bothered me (and still does) that I have to ask what's being said around me and when I get a response, sometimes the content gets lost in the translation. I decided to try and change that. I enrolled in an entry-level class at the local community college, only to encounter more disappointment. Most of the students in the class were Tagalog-speaking Filipinos and took the class for an easy "A." The teacher went with the flow of the majority of the class and within a few weeks I fell behind. It seemed that I was the only one in this position and I ended up dropping the class.

There were of course some people that I met who were helpful in teaching me Tagalog. I worked at a company with a group of Filipinos who were friendly and understanding about my situation. My cubicle had an eraser board and every so often my co-workers would say something to me in Tagalog, then wrote it on the board to help me remember. It gave me a little practice and I was happy that they didn't judge my upbringing or me.

Fast forward to the present. I am now married to a man who is a first generation American-born Filipino, who was raised in a Filipino household where Tagalog was spoken, and where he and his siblings and most of his relatives understand the language. So of course I have found myself in tons of situations where his parents or relatives are telling a story in Tagalog and I have no clue whatsoever to what's being said. My husband translates when I ask what's going on. Yet I continue to get frustrated, feel left out, and am sometimes embarrassed to always have to ask what's being said. There are times when I joke and say, "English please," and everyone laughs, then they translate, but I still wish I could just understand.

A few years ago I took a trip to the Philippines to attend the wedding of a friend. I figured I could try to learn some basic words, so I rented an audio CD from the local library. I was able to learn a few phrases while listening in my car driving to and from work. My husband also bought me an entry-level interactive language program to help me learn a little more from the convenience of our home. It's fun and easy to use and I plan to purchase the next level to further my language skills. Maybe one day I'll be able to get through an entire Filipino movie and understand all the conversation.

Almost all of my Filipino friends who are first generation born in the U.S. understand Tagalog. I am thankful that they are able to teach me some words here and there. Every little bit helps.

To this day, I still struggle with the language. I still get frustrated when I find myself in a situation where I'm the only one in the group that does not understand. Sometimes I wish there were more Filipino culture and language classes offered when I was a child. It is great to see that there are more options these days to try and learn any language—from physical classes to learning from your computer. My goal is to learn enough Tagalog so that I can at least get the gist of the conversations going on around me. Then hopefully I won't have to utter the words "*hindi ako nakakaintindi*" (I do not understand) as often!

WHISPER, CARABAO

Tony Robles

Not long ago I saw an interview with a Filipino writer who spoke of clichés that Filipino writers—mostly beginning Filipino writers—use. He cited such things as mango colored suns, white sand beaches and, of course, the obligatory carabao as hindrances to the literary landscape one is trying to create. This writer's comments made me think of my own writing and the role the carabao has played in it. Firstly, I have never seen a carabao in person. The carabao is a beautiful animal—hard working and loyal—I've been told. The people who have told me this of the carabao also happen to be hard working and loyal (and I have been told that I have displayed just the opposite qualities, namely by my father). I have seen the carabao in pictures—*National Geographic* and in numerous books showing the landscape of my indigenous ancestral home, the Philippines. I felt somewhat guilty in regards to the writer's comments because I had used carabaos and mango colored skies as metaphors in my writing. "You're a sham," a friend once told me. "You've never seen a carabao in your life, nor have you been to the Philippines." This was true. But I began to think about the writer, who is quite well known since the release of his book, which has been well-received. I looked at his face, his clothes, his hair—all were immaculate, all impurities swept away in the Archipelago winds. I was curious if this writer had ever stepped into a steaming mound of carabao dung in his oxfords or boat shoes and subsequently fallen. Or did he ever wake to find carabao crust in his eyes, or walk with carabao mud between his toes or carabao snots running down his nose? These and other questions remain—the mystery persists.

My uncle, the poet Al Robles, wrote of carabaos. His book of poems, *Rappin' With Ten Thousand Carabaos In the Dark* are carabao tracks on the page, tracing their journey in the Philippines and in the United States. Each poem is stained with the mud, saliva, tears, *tae*—the life of the carabao, the memory of the carabao, the music of the carabao—the heart of the carabao which is the heart of the *manongs*. The sound of the carabao brings us closer to home, closer to the earth, closer to ourselves. Carlos Bulosan wrote of the carabao in *America Is in the Heart*. In the story, his brother Amado beats a weary carabao with a stick, to which his father responds by slapping him sharply across the face, "What are you doing to the carabao?" I think of one of my uncle's poems and the reverence he had for the carabao:

> *He's nice one, you know*
> *Carabao is nice to you*
> *When you come in the afternoon from the ricefield*
> *He go home too, by himself*
> *After the sun go down he lay down*
> *Goddam! Like a human being.*
> *International Hotel Night Watch*
> *Manong—carabao*
> *I ride you thru the I-Hotel ricefields*
> *One by one the carabao plows deep*

I recently took a walk to the grocery store in my neighborhood. I picked up a few things and headed back home. A couple of blocks away from my house I came upon a garage sale. I approached and saw the usual—books, plates, clothes, knickknacks—all kinds of stuff. It all belonged to a young white guy wearing a Giants T-shirt. His face had a pinkish tint due to the unusually hot weather. He sipped on a Pabst Blue Ribbon as people browsed through the items making up his life. I looked at a few things but didn't see anything I wanted to buy. I was ready to leave when something caught my eye. It was on a table, a wooden figure that looked worn but beautiful, crafted by someone I'd never met but whose feelings I'd feel as my own. I reached for and touched the figure. Its eyes whispered. I tried to make out what it was saying but was interrupted by the guy with the beer. "You like my yak?" he asked before taking a swig of beer. He took a very long swig before proceeding to crush the empty can with one squeeze of his freckled hand. He stood examining my face. I looked at the wooden figure and realized it was a carabao. It was beautiful. It had eyes that were alive. But before I could tell the garage sale guy that what he had was a carabao, not a yak, he went to the cooler and pulled out another beer. He walked back over and told me that his yak had belonged to his ex-wife, who had gotten the lion's share in the divorce. He made fun of the yak, saying it needed another yak to fuck (a yak to yuk, to use his exact words), etc. I looked at the carabao, it looked at me. We knew. Then the man started rambling about this and that—a rant of belligerence mixed with a twinge of sentimentality, his words spilling forth in a spirited froth of beverage-inspired verbiage. As I recall, it went like this:

Yak yak yak yak yak yak yak yak yak yak yak yak yak yak yak yak yak yak yak yak

Yak yak....yak yak yak...yak yak yak yak...yak yak yak yak yak

Yak yak yak yak yak yak yak yak yak yak yak yak yak yak yak yak yak yak yak

Yak yak yak yak yak yak yak yak yak yak yak yak yak yak yak yak yak yak yak

Yak yak yak yak yak yak yak yak yak yak yak yak yak yak yak yak

Tony Robles

yak yak yak yak yak
Yakitty yak
Kayak

He yakked my head off for almost half an hour. Finally he stopped. Then I uttered two words:
How much?

Five bucks

I dug into my pocket and the carabao seemed to say: "If you don't get me out of here and away from this fool, I'm gonna back up and run as fast as I can, dead at you, and ram one of my horns up your ass."

I found five dollars, gave it to the guy and picked up the carabao that had to endure being called a yak for who knows how long.

I brought it home where it belonged.

A VISIT TO GRANDPA'S HOUSE

Jeanine Silverio

Peaches, walnuts, and sweet potatoes stood in silent rows, watching my procession. The sickly sweet smell of decaying fruit filled my nostrils. With no other car for miles around, I gunned the accelerator of the light blue Malibu. Magnolia Avenue. My grandparents' house would be up ahead.

What was once a busy, bustling migrant farm was now a lonely, echoing ghost town. No old *manongs* sitting under the ancient walnut tree, no men in the pool hall hustling money on the tables. A broken screen door banged heavily against a rotting doorframe. The stairs of the workers' bunkhouse hung listlessly against the outside wall. Dragonflies droned lazily by the empty garage.

The house itself had fallen into disrepair. Pale green paint peeled from the walls. The windows were dark with grime. Grandma's once-prized flower garden lay dead and brown under the blistering sun.

I parked the car, went into the Big Kitchen, the kitchen where Grandpa used to make meals for all the migrant workers before and after a long day's work in the surrounding fields. The long rows of tables were empty now, the floor coated with a film of sand. Flies struggled in dusty cobwebs in the window. But one thing hadn't changed: The delicious aroma of Grandpa's *adobo* and *tanghun* wafted from the covered pots.

Grandpa stood there, his "Sweet Potato Joe" hat perched on his white hair. He saw me and a smile lit up his features.

"Denging! My Denging! What are you doing here?"

"I'm visiting for a while, Grandpa."

Just then, one of the Mexican workers trudged into the kitchen, his shoulders sagging as if in defeat. Grandpa shuffled over to see what he needed. The Mexican held a check in his hand and spoke to Grandpa in broken English.

"What?" Grandpa asked.

The Mexican repeated his request.

"What?"

The Mexican handed over the check. Grandpa took the check, first turning it one way and then the other. He looked over at me, puzzled.

"He wants to know if you would cash the check, Grandpa."

Grandpa still stared at the check with a look of bewilderment. The Mexican waited expectantly. Finally, I looked at the check he held in his hands.

It was upside down.

Gently, I reached over and turned the check for him

"It says three-hundred and eighty-six dollars, Grandpa."

"Oh. We cannot give cash for you."

The Mexican nodded, took the check, and left.

Grandpa turned back to me. His hands were gnarled, calloused. The lines in his face had deepened. Or had I just never noticed? This stooped man had emigrated from the Philippines when he was twenty years old to seek a better life in America. He labored in the sugar cane plantations of Hawaii before settling in California to work the fields. He formed a huge Filipino migrant camp at a time when Filipino field workers were looked upon with hatred and prejudice. He had fought for better working conditions for "his boys" in the fields, and helped form one of the first agricultural unions for Filipinos. He had raised eight children. And now, he was old.

"Where you stay?" he asked.

"I'm staying at Auntie Auring's and Adele's house."

"When you get here?"

"Friday."

"Friday? And you just come now to see me?"

"I didn't have a car, Grandpa," I explained lamely.

"Well, you stay here tonight. Go back tomorrow."

"I can't Grandpa. I have to bring the car back."

"Oh. You mebbe come this weekend."

"Okay."

"Did you eat? You eat something."

I smiled. Usually, that's the first thing to come out of his mouth. His toothless smile met mine.

I heaped a plate full of steaming rice and chicken. We ate in the living room and watched game shows. He settled back in his old, green recliner. It didn't seem so long ago that he would pick me up and sit me in the chair with him until I fell asleep, my thumb stuck in my mouth. Or when he would take me out to the pig sty, lift me up and let me throw the sweet potatoes to the grunting pigs.

Then, it was time for me to leave.

"I've got to go now, Grandpa."

"Already? You just got here."

"I know, but Adele's expecting me back."

"You stay with me this weekend, huh?"

"Yeah. I'll be here Saturday for sure."

I spent the rest of the day with Adele, giggling, playing records, looking at magazines. We spent the night smashing grasshoppers in their little grocery store.

The phone rang the next morning, pulling me out of a dreamless sleep. I stumbled my way to the phone.

"Hello?" I croaked into the receiver.

Jeanine Silverio

Someone mumbled into the phone.
"What?"
Again, I heard the mumbling.
"What?!!"
"I said, this is Gabriel! Grandpa's dead."

FILIPINO AMERICAN IDENTITY: A TEENAGER'S EXPERIENCE

Adrian James Sobredo

*T*eens are typically known to rebel against their elders to find their own identity and find out who they are. Unlike most teenagers, I seem to be drawn to my elders and I am discovering this is not such a bad way to go about forming one's identity.

I am sixteen years old. I was born in Stockton, California, a Filipino American heartland in the 1930s and 1940s. I have lived and attended schools in Stockton, San Francisco, Los Angeles, and Davis, all in California.

I spent my early teen years in predominantly white schools. How did I do it? What helped me deal with and express my Filipino identity among Asian American friends who did not quite know what to make of it? How has my experience changed now that I am attending a high school in Stockton? This is my story.

I spent three years of junior high school in Davis, California, a predominantly white community.

In Harper Junior High School in 2006-2009, the student body was about 65 percent white.

Ironically, the school was named after an accomplished black poet, born free, and who helped educate freed slaves—Frances Ellen Harper.

In the three years at Harper, I have met only two other Filipinos and one of them was half-Austrian. Records showed there were four students who identified themselves as Filipino/Filipino American in a school of over 750 students. My closest friend was a Chinese American who moved from China at a very young age. My Chinese American friend attended Chinese language school. He wondered why I didn't go to Chinese language school on Saturdays like he did. He said I couldn't relate because I wasn't Asian.

I said, "I am Asian, I'm Filipino." He sounded clueless, then recovered and said, "Well... that's the fake Asian." I didn't find his comment surprising, as Asians often could not tell my ethnicity but what had not happened to me before being told that Filipinos aren't Asians.

I argued with him that the Philippines is in Asia. My friend simply believed that the countries most recognized as being Asian were the powerhouses like China, Japan, and India. This is where he said I was not one of the "main Asians."

I was not shaken by the whole experience. I didn't even think it was an insult or even a conversation worth remembering. I was just thinking about how close-minded my friend was. I already knew he wasn't right and admittedly had problems of his own at home. My father heard this phone conversation in the car when he picked me up from school. I repeated the conversation to my mother. My parents were a little worried for me and wondered if I felt okay about the comment. I really hadn't known I was anything else but Filipino.

Before moving to Davis, I attended Merryhill School at Brookside in Stockton. In 3rd grade I was able to proudly state that I was Filipino and could impress everyone for knowing such a long word. I guess I did tend to be the only Filipino in the classroom. In 6th grade, everyone in the upper grades knew everyone. People from Merryhill School remember me today when we became reacquainted in high school. But Harper had a much larger student body, about 750 as opposed to Merryhill's 200 plus kids attending kindergarten to 8th grade. Harper was my first public school experience. It was also where I experienced questions about my ethnic identity.

Most of the time, I cannot guess the ethnicities of my classmates at a glance, by the skin tone, or even when given a full name. If faces show similarities to any of my relatives, then I might think they are Filipinos. In my first year at Harper, I definitely wasn't looking for any Filipino kid in a new campus. That was not a top priority. I worried more about figuring out who I could trust and connect with. I had to make a new group of friends for the first time since 1st grade.

I went once to a very special evening event at Konditorei, an Austrian pastry cafe and restaurant that my parents were familiar with. It was to celebrate the owners' 15 years of business in Davis. I was treated to a very unique tasting and probably some of the best pastries and European food I ever had. It turns out that the couple who owns the restaurant is an Austrian Pastry Chef and his Filipina wife who was a former ballerina in Vienna, and their daughter was a fellow student at Harper. That was my Filipino contact in Davis.

Yes, I was born in Stockton, America's Filipino town, but I grew up where I had no Filipino neighbors. I attended schools where Filipino presence was small. Despite all that, growing up I was often exposed to very prominent Filipinos and Filipino Americans.

Sadly, I never knew much about NVM Gonzalez, a famous Filipino fiction writer, or Al Robles, a famous Filipino American poet, until recently. But I was around them both most of my young life. I have seen photos of me at 4 years old with NVM Gonzalez. My father told me the photos were taken in Los Angeles. NVM was serving as the UC Regents' Professor at the University of California at Los Angeles (UCLA) in 1998. I know now that NVM was named the National Artist for Literature of the Republic of the Philippines in 1997. In 1998, he also received the Philippines' Centennial Award for Literature. NVM died in 1999 so I missed out on thoughtful conversations about life or about being a Filipino writer in America. Still I am fortunate that whenever I want to hear stories of the times my father spent in discussions with NVM, I can.

Al Robles also appears in my family photos. One picture was of my moth-

Adrian James Sobredo

pushing me in a stroller when I was barely 2 years old, marching with Al. My parents told me the picture was taken in 1996 during a candlelight rally where supporters walked from Market Street to a fenced-off hole in the ground that used to be the old International Hotel. The rally was to keep the hope alive of rebuilding the I-Hotel in San Francisco. Al is also gone now. He died in 2009, but he got to see the new I-Hotel become a reality. I learned more about the impact that Al Robles had on the Filipino community at his memorial service at Glide Memorial than all those times I'd seen him in person. Maybe because I am a little older, the elders in the Filipino community are growing older or dying, and there is urgency that I pay more attention.

I remember going to an event at the I-Hotel and being in awe at the photography exhibits and the poetry. It was a tribute for Al Robles. This happened about a year before he died. It makes me more proud to be Filipino thinking about that event. A multicultural crowd came to honor and celebrate Al's life and his contribution to the Filipino American community. I don't think he liked the limelight as he stood in the back throughout the event.

I know that there are Filipinos like NVM, Al Robles and many others who celebrate being Filipino and Filipino Americans. I think about that when people at Harper called the Philippines "the Mexico of Asia." In general, they most likely meant it in a derogatory way. So seeing that there are so many people celebrating who we are outweighs those comments from middle school.

What else helped me express being Filipino? During my 8th Grade American Studies class at Harper, I had a young teacher who encouraged us to be creative. It was my teacher's idea to ask our parents what they would recommend us to read for our independent reading assignment. My teacher encouraged the idea of writing a story about Filipinos during the Great Depression. My father recommended that I read *America Is in the Heart* by Carlos Bulosan. There were multiple copies in the house as my father used this book as a required reading in a college course he taught at Sacramento State

University. His students also had the option of taking tours of Little Manila for extra credit.

The book became more real to me when my father pointed out places in Stockton that were mentioned in the book. Some examples were the downtown, Little Manila, and the Daguhoy Lodge where we practice *Filipino Martial Arts*. The story is also similar to my great-grandfather's experiences in America as a migrant farm worker.

When I was young, about 7 years old in Stockton, my father wanted me to learn martial arts. This way he wouldn't have to worry about me if mugged when I'm older and maybe increase my chances of defending myself against a psycho with a knife. It just so happens that my father became good friends with a Filipino martial arts grandmaster, Tony Somera. Since I started so young, perhaps there were hopes of me becoming a highly skilled member of the group when I became older. But I actually advanced through the system quite slowly. Then I moved to Davis and didn't have the time to commute every Saturday. This all changed when we moved back to Stockton to attend St. Mary's High School starting my sophomore year in 2009.

I am attending St. Mary's High School as a junior in the Fall 2010. St. Mary's is also where Uncle Fred Cordova, co-founder of the Filipino American National Historical Society (FANHS), attended high school in Stockton, a few decades earlier. Saint Mary's student body is more diverse than Harper in Davis. The student body of about 1,100 is 51 percent White, and 49 percent mixture of African Americans, Asians, Hispanics, and Native Americans. I actually have met several students who are Filipino. One of them is a distant relative. I also have gotten positive feedback when I am among my Filipino friends for just mentioning eating some Filipino food—banana *turon*, chicken *adobo* and *ube hopia*.

Being at St. Mary's and in Stockton allowed me to return to Filipino Martial Arts and I actually enjoy practicing more than before, especially under the tutelage of Grandmaster Tony Somera and Master Joel Juanitas. I also appreciate the history of both the art and the Daguhoy Lodge. I have more opportunities to help out with our demonstrations at community events. I can actually be a part of the Barrio Fiesta, the Obon Festival and others. The Obon Festival is a pretty good deal—with a promise of some free roasted chicken for participating.

At the Daguhoy Lodge, I listen intently to Grandmaster Somera telling new students and guests about the history of Bahala Na Martial Arts, that the late Sgt. Leo Giron, a Filipino American veteran of World War II, created it. Every time Grandmaster Somera tells the story, it becomes a confirmation that I play a part in supporting and continuing the art that Grandmaster Leo started.

My experiences may not be the same as that of my maternal great-grandfather, Perfecto de los Santos, who came to America during the Great Depression and worked as a farm laborer, or that of my father, James Sobredo, who grew up in a poor family in Guam in the 1960s. Both my father and my maternal great-grandfather lived with communities made up of mostly Filipinos. My great-grandfather came to America from the Philippines when he was 24 years old in the beginning of the Great Depression. He already had a solid identity of being Filipino and lived and worked in a community of Filipinos in California as a farm laborer. During off-season in California, he worked with other Filipinos in the fish canneries in Alaska.

My father grew up in a poor Filipino community in Guam, an American territory on an Island of mostly Chamorros. My father had a solid Filipino identity because in his community, their identity was never in question. At the famous college prep school he attended in Guam, his group of friends even called themselves the "Tagalog Gang," just for fun; none of their families were from the Tagalog region of the Philippines. And they weren't even a street gang. One of my dad's classmates is now the Governor of Guam and another is now Supreme Court Justice in Guam.

The major difference in growing up Filipino in America for me is that I didn't have the same community of Filipinos in my everyday life. I have never had Filipino neighbors. As a teenager, my school communities, both in private and public schools, are predominantly White. In spite of this, I am growing up knowing I am Filipino and thanks to my elders, I am learning and appreciating so much more about the Filipino American experiences in the United States of America.

I may not know fully yet what having a Filipino American identity is like. All I know is that my Filipino American identity is important to me and is a work in progress just like me.

BLACKAPINA
THIRD MOVEMENT: THE BLEND
(An excerpt from *Midnight Peaches, Two O'clock Patience*)

Janet Stickmon

*B*eing both African-American and Filipino-American means having the benefit of drawing from the richness of both ethnicities and bearing the responsibility of sharing both ethnicities with all I come in contact with. It means understanding and living out the complex interplay between culture, race, and ethnicity on a daily basis. Throughout my life, I was constantly searching for a word or label that would communicate my pride in both sides. Identifying as only African-American or Filipino-American never felt right because it just wasn't true. College and scholarship applications told me, "Please choose one," but categories like African-American and Asian/Pacific Islander felt too constraining. Friends, family, and strangers frequently asked me, "Are you more Filipino than Black or more Black than Filipino," questions that reflect a dangerous polarization and discomfort with nuance. Such binary thinking dictates how many of us operating in a Western context tend to approach people and ideas; we are conditioned to choose between or identify with one of two extremes—black and white, rich and poor, good and evil—suggesting that one couldn't possibly: 1) identify with more than one thing at the same time, 2) embrace a perspective or state of being somewhere in between, or 3) have multiple options to choose from other than the two presented.

Though such things were limiting, I never felt so frustrated by racial categories or questions reflecting binary thought that I longed to identify as "just human." This didn't fully capture what I was about either, especially since being both Black and Filipina shaped my human experience. My humanity was not something that could be extracted from its ethnic milieu. I was one who valued the unique histories of both sides and wanted to celebrate how being African-American and Filipina-American have shaped my human experience.

For many years I identified as half Black and half Filipino, figuring this was a way I could declare to the world that I was both. However, identifying in terms of fractions reinforced a fragmented self-perception; it signified my silent insecurity about believing I was a diluted or counterfeit version of each ethnicity. Since my Filipino features weren't immediately noticeable to most people in Lancaster, CA, I became aware that phenotypically I looked Black and therefore regularly reminded others that I was also Filipino, being sure to use the few Cebuano words I knew. Throughout my childhood and adolescent years, I did this partly to show pride in my Filipino side, but also to show myself off as not-your-average-Black-person—someone with an "interesting" twist. I discovered that I received more attention when people learned I was mixed—not necessarily always good attention. So as early as elementary school, long before I had the language for it, I had done what many had done to me: I exoticized myself. I continued to do so until I became aware of some direct consequences of exoticization—not always feeling special and unique in a positive sense, but instead feeling freakish and less human.

During my late teens and early twenties, I noticed that I felt pressured to believe I had to turn on and off each side of my ethnic identity depending on who was around. I thought that in order to be accepted as Black within an all Black social environment, I had to "turn on" my Black side (whatever that meant) and leave behind or downplay my Filipino side; when I was in an all Filipino environment I felt that I had to "turn on" my Filipino-ness (whatever that meant) and downplay my Black side. I felt like I was contextualizing; however, this wasn't satisfying and I continued to search for a way to contextualize without denying my other half. I wanted to bring all of me wherever I went, and I wanted all of me to be accepted regardless of whose company I was in.

Making attempts to be in touch with both sides, learning about the history of both and remaining socially connected to each community, I eventually became comfortable saying I was 100% African-American and 100% Filipino-American and devised various combinations of these terms. I was and am fully both. Identifying as such seemed to be a defiant response to the questions, "Are you more Filipino than Black? More Black than Filipino?" Not only was I proud to be both, but I was also proud to be a woman. So, beginning in my late twenties, I found ways to embrace my womanhood as I bounced between several ways of identifying: Filipino-African-American woman. African-Filipino-American woman. Filipina-African-American. African-Filipina-American. These names communicated the ideas of "together" and "distinct" at the same time.

In early 2007, the possibility of identifying as "Blackapino" or "Blackapina" crossed my mind. The term floated around in my head for a bit, but didn't seem to get concretized for quite some time. I didn't have the courage to use it, but I couldn't completely articulate why. In retrospect, I know some of this had to do with my discomfort with blending terms, as if the process of blending would corrupt the ethnic essence of each side. This was an indication that I was still afraid of being viewed as a diluted version of a Filipina or African-American. I was also hesitant to use the term because to untutored ears it evoked only laughter and was never taken seriously; hidden in the laughter, I could almost hear people say, "Aw, that's cute and catchy. But is that real? Is that a real, lived experience?"

Folded into this transition were memories of a number of young scholars who published articles on multiracial identity. Among these scholars who inspired me to reconsider the concept of blending and blended terms (like Mexipino and Blaxican) were Rudy Guevarra, Jr., Rebecca Romo, and Matthew M. Andrews.

What brought it all together for me was the work of Susan Leksander who applied the concept of psychosynthesis to multiracial clients. Leksander's research helped me understand both of my ethnicities as being among the several subpersonalities that could be fully integrated into my sense of self—and this would be normal, not weird, and not pathological.

My nucleus of subpersonalities was and will continue to be strengthened by my continuous immersion in social circles consisting of African-Americans, Filipino-Americans, women, introverts, extroverts, artists, athletes, theologians, healers, the various subgroups lying within each circle, and the intersection of all these and more. This nucleus is a tight, yet fluid, ever-expansive, ever-evolving blend housed within my spirit. I possess an authenticity that laughs in the face of essentialism. I am "Blackapina." Black. Filipino-American. Woman. I am an African-American unafraid of identifying as Black because it hearkens back to the Black Power Movement when Black, the color and the culture, were embraced with pride. I am a second-generation Filipina-American, holding my mother's immigrant dreams and sacrifices; as my *utang na loob*, I offer Momma and Daddy the fruits of my work as professor of Filipina(o)-American Heritage and Africana Studies. I am a woman who menstruates and gives birth and nurses and nurtures and fights. I am each of these and more. I am all these at the same time. I live at the crossroads, straddling multiple worlds. Hybridity is my home where transition and nuance are always welcome. At the interstices, you'll hear my breath. When I walk, listen for the sound of ancestral spirits and deities hailing from the African continent and the Philippine Islands; hear them pulse and drift, cry and whisper, laugh and pray as they clear the way for their children to walk the world protected, guided, and strengthened.

I am one of those children who walks the world protected by these spirits. My four-year-old daughter also walks enshrouded in their guidance. My husband and I try our best to encourage her to embrace all of her ethnicities; not only is she African-American and Filipina-American, but she is also Jamaican and Puerto Rican. This is a challenge, but one that we welcome since we know she will benefit from the richness of all four ethnicities in the same way I have benefitted from both of mine. From the food, stories, and songs to the languages, people, and cultural events, our daughter will learn and be at peace with the beauty of the multiplicity that exists within herself and within the world.

I AM AN AMERICAN

Clifton Trinidad

"Where you from? I mean where are you 'really' from?" I get this all the time here in America. I have spent a major part of my adult life overseas in really cool places and in some dirt holes during the 23 years I served in the Army. But overseas, especially in Europe, that was a rare question. My language, mannerisms, and dress clearly gave away that I was an American. Even where there are a lot of other Filipinos—like in Italy or Germany—it is always evident. When you grow up in America, for sure it shows. In the Army it was rare that I was asked where I was from, and if I was asked it was usually due to my California "dude" accent. When another Filipino asks this question, rarely do they get it right, and they ask this question a lot. Many thought I was Japanese or some unusual mix of Hispanic because I was a tad hairier in the face. It's like, I know you but you don't know me kind of a thing. I know they are Pinoy, but they don't know that I am. Another soldier, born in the Philippines, got technical and said, "No, you are a brown American."

    I joined the Army with no particular purpose. I went in as a private, became a sergeant, spent time as a Chief Warrant Officer, and retired as a Major. It is possible for the son of a steward to break the mold. The time spent in the military was not without issues. If my rank was hidden, I was often asked directions to the mess hall. Once on board a contracted military flight, I was asked by the stewardess if I spoke English. She was promptly embarrassed when I informed her that I did speak English as well as the men in the twenty rows behind me who were flying with me. To set another picture of issues, I was asked politely if I would wear a Japanese Army uniform for display of artifacts and got my picture taken. I think it still hangs in the Infantry Museum at Fort Benning, Georgia.

My parents are both American. My dad was born in 1910 in the Philippines and came to the states in the '20s. He worked in the Salinas Valley, Los Angeles, and San Francisco. He was a U.S. national when he came over via a long ride on a ship. He served his country in the First Filipino Infantry Regiment in Australia, New Guinea, and the Philippines. The Army formalized his citizenship, I believe it was at Camp Roberts, California. I think his brother, also in the First Filipino Infantry, was killed in New Guinea in 1942. I once asked my father about this and he never answered. I never asked again. He was proud of being an Infantryman and never failed to rag on one of my uncles who was "supply." My mom was a war bride. She was also from the Philippines and became a citizen in the late '50s.

I am a post-war child and I have two brothers that I know of. Being post-war born, if I have other siblings, I do not really know. Many of my dad's friends and cousins have pre-war children from local women, and my family is a mix of Hispanic, Native American (Chumash), Italian, and Irish. I was born in San Francisco at Children's Hospital on Geary Street in the mid-1950s. I grew up mostly in San Francisco and lived on Austin Alley, Divisadero, Grove, Haight, and Page streets. I attended Morning Star Catholic School, Andrew Jackson, Dudley Stone, Herbert Hoover, and am a graduate of "the" Polytechnic High School, class of Fall '72, not a transplant to McAteer. I graduated from San Francisco City College and San Francisco State University. Yup, I went to SF State back in the '70s, a time of self-exploration, struggle, partying, and some serious hanging out. I also lived in San Diego and Oxnard but that is another story.

Growing up was a bit painful. At the elementary schools I attended, I was usually the only Filipino American in class. This often led to problems that had me in the principal's office more than I liked to have been. I was prone to having a smart mouth, quick temper, and was quite fond of flipping the bird. Even now, I am fond of that digital signature. Later, my mom and dad divorced and suddenly there was no male figure to "get the belt" from. We ended up on welfare and I found myself having to defend my mother's honor, so to speak. Kids my age were prone to saying things like, "Yo momma's on welfare," which earned a fight and a subsequent seat in the principal's office.

Both my mom's and my dad's family pretty much just turned their backs and ignored us for years. I did have three uncles: Eddie Trinidad, Andy and Danny Evangelista, who kept an eye on me and did stay in touch. I am in perpetual debt to them for this.

Later, Mom remarried my stepfather who was from Central America. He was a mix of Coastal Hispanic, which is a little bit of Indian, a little bit of white, some Hispanic and the rest mostly black from Honduras. The majority of his family is black from the "Filmo," the Fillmore District in the City (San Francisco). My black cousins, all considerably larger than me, usually took care of any "issues" that were bigger than me in the neighborhood with other kids. These issues were the same as before: fighting, being a smartass, and being an overall pain in school. My cousins loved my mom and her cooking immensely. I am the odd-man-out at family gatherings on the Honduran side and trust me, though I do look different, for years this was the only family I had, and I did fit in. No one questioned my heritage within the family. It has always been family first. There is no color here.

My dad came back into my life as he got older. He had spent a vast amount of time traveling and at sea. One day he was aboard a ship off the coast of Viet Nam, the next week he was back in the City. He had retired from sea service close to the age of sixty. I was already 19 or 20 at the time and already at City College. His generation–the greatest–are now gone and I miss him every day of my life. His generation faced an enormity of adversity, and he paved the way for me and my brother. My dad filled me in on things I did not know about, like who was related to us and how. He managed to fill in all the blanks to the questions I had, not only about his family, like who were his cousins and who was really an uncle and who was just a friend, but also who my godparents were.

Today, in my immediate family there are just a handful of us left, and we can't even fill up a living room. It's just me and my two brothers and a few cousins. Going home is always hard. Many of my friends are still doing the same old thing they were doing when I left for the service and are really unchanged, just looking older, and time was not kind to some of them. I tell you, this is most hard to comprehend. Parents gone, uncles and aunts gone, streets changed, even sports stadiums have changed. Who remembers Kezar Pavilion, and the Warriors Basketball Arena on Turk or O'Farrell Streets? It's hard and I don't torture myself. I rarely go home now.

Being me has never been easy and it is not easy now. After all these years I still have elements of conflict and self-doubt. I am still a bit of a misfit in many respects, but, I can say I do know who I am. I define myself as an American of Filipino ancestry, Filipino-American. I have always been proud of my heritage. I know my history, my family and their experiences in America and in the Philippines. I don't deny or reject, or defer anything. I was born here, grew up here, and served my country. Like I am going to live elsewhere? I have visited the Philippines on various occasions, and have no great reason to live there. Home really is the United States, San Francisco—America, dude. If anybody asks if I am an American, my answer is, well of course I am!

MY GAY FATHER AND THE SUPREME COURT

Nikki Vilas

My name is Nikki Vilas. I live in Lafayette, California. I don't know how to share this story to the people that I believe need to understand. Between my mother and me, we have exercised the right to marry six times. I wish I could say the same for my sister who is gay. I don't brag about my marriages and the subsequent failure of the previous two, only to make the point that I could get married, while my sister, who was in a committed relationship for twenty years, raised a son together, could not exercise that right. I believe what may make the story of my family interesting is that my sisters and I were raised by our gay father and his partner from the time we were three, five, and six respectively, and are now well into our 50s. Our father's name is Hank Vilas. He can be seen in a documentary called *Before Stonewall* which highlights gay life in the early 1900s through the 1960s. Our father reviewed our homework, nursed us when we were sick, never missed important and not so important events in our lives until the day he died. I do not profess to be a writer but felt this story needed to be told.

My friend said to me today that this is the time, if ever there was, to share this story. This week the Supreme Court has a decision to make that will have a tremendous impact on a community that can no longer be ignored. They are your relatives, your co-workers, your neighbors, your friends and acquaintances.

I was born in Berkeley, California in 1954. I have two sisters. Our mother is Filipina and Black and our father was Caucasian of Scots-Irish descent. Our father came from a very strict Republican upbringing and was characteristically disowned for about eight years when he married our mother.

They married about one year after the law prohibiting interracial marriages was overturned in California. They found themselves migrating to Berkeley where a community of "misfits" found safe harbor from the bigotry surrounding them at that time. I don't remember much of my mother and father's marriage, as they were divorced when I was about five years old, when my father could no longer deny that he was a homosexual. He tells that story in the documentary *Before Stonewall*. Dad had fallen in love with Bob who moved in shortly after our parents were divorced. He and Bob, whom I affectionately call Mom, were together for twenty years.

My sisters and I grew up in Berkeley and were in our formative years in the latter '60s and '70s. To not be against the Vietnam War, not fight for Civil Rights, and not be a feminist was anti-Berkeley. I sang every Joan Baez song she ever sang, marched in anti-war marches, and would have burned my bra if I could find one that fit a size double A. What we didn't know to fight for were gay rights. From the time I was five, we spent every weekend with Dad and Bob. The father always got weekend custody in those times.

For us, Dad and Bob were our safe haven, the fun home. Now I understand that much of what we loved about Dad and Bob is now a stereotype and a cliché. While Dad was a social welfare worker by trade, he was in a little theater group called the Jack London Circle Players. He and Bob played the fathers in *The Fantastics* in the mid-1960s, a play to this day in which I wanted to play the girl with them in their roles as the fathers. At home, Dad would often play the piano and we would gather around and sing show tunes at the top of our lungs. To us, this loving home was normal. We did not know otherwise until we were teenagers and realized that it was probably only in Berkeley that we could be truthful about our parents.

In our father's house, Dad was always the dad and Bob, if he had a role, was the mom. He was the better cook and cared about décor and fashion.

Nikki Vilas

When I was about nineteen, I saw a French movie called *La Cage Aux Folles* and was stunned at the similarities in our lives! Later, *Bird Cage* came out, the American version of the French film. I found it difficult to watch as I kept thinking that Robin Williams—whose role seemed closer to my Dad's—was too remorseful and sad and Nathan Lane, whom I saw as Bob, was too campy and over the top. While Bob was not a drag queen, as is the Nathan Lane character in the film, he would brag about his size 14 feet and say how great his legs looked in a nice pair of stilettos.

Our father had an economics degree from Stanford, went to Cal Berkeley at forty, where he picked up his Master's degree in Social Welfare. When he retired, he volunteered as a counselor for gay, lesbian, and transgenders at the Pacific Center in Berkeley, a center that caters to alternative lifestyle, health and well-being. He belonged to Mensa but bragged that it was the gay Mensa. He raised us to believe that education was critical to our future success, well in advance of the norm at the time. Our father loved us unconditionally.

I remember when he told me he was gay. I was seventeen. I recall he hesitated, but when he did tell me I laughed and told him I already knew. I actually had known since I was about thirteen when my mother told me and my older sister confirmed. I did not know at thirteen what homosexuality was. When my mother told me, she and my stepfather were having difficulties, so it was told to me with a negative slant that I did not understand. My father subsequently wrote a beautiful letter to his brother that he shared with us that mentions the moment when he told me and what he felt at the time. This is an excerpt from that letter:

> "Since I fully accept myself and therefore rather expected everyone else to accept me, my arrangement with Bob was always pretty open. Since I didn't know what peer group pressures the girls were under however, I didn't discuss it with them. Bob, who is considerably more tied up than I am, actually made diverting noises. I nevertheless assumed that they knew

Nikki Vilas

I was gay. I had a long talk with Nikki last year, however, and found that this wasn't the case and they didn't know it until about three years earlier. At that time, their mother, who was very upset by the girls' premature sexuality (by the standards of our generation) told them all about their father's 'sexuality problems.' As is evident my respect, admiration, and love for my three daughters know no bounds. In addition to their obvious individual assets, their beautiful acceptance of me and my lifestyle may help explain my feelings towards them."

It is interesting growing up in Berkeley. You are, on the one hand, enlightened, and on the other, sheltered and naïve. I could tell my friends my parents were gay, but I found myself hiding this truth to those I would meet in the world who I could not trust would understand. While our father was open and honest, Bob had reason to stay in the closet to his co-workers. He asked that we respect his feelings and privacy on the matter as he was subject to a great deal of bigotry and hatred. For years I found myself guarding the "secret" of our family while openly embracing the love and uniqueness of it all. Funny how even those who claim they are open still would remark how our father didn't "act" gay. All I could say was, "have you met my mom?"

Our father died of AIDS in 1985. He was sixty. I miss him to this day. He never hesitated to tell his friends, and us, how much he loved his daughters. My sisters and I nursed him at a time when people were afraid to breathe the air of someone afflicted with this terrible disease. We watched him waste away with a bravery and humor I hope to have when it is my time. He loved us and we loved him to the end. While Bob and Dad had split up a few years before he died, Bob was his soul mate. He was the first person I called when Dad died and Bob helped us get through the loss with the same humor he shared with our father.

A very good friend of mine said girls look to marry their fathers. As I was arguing the logic behind that statement I realized I couldn't do half bad if I married someone like my dad. He was funny, smart, loving, and nurturing.

I don't know that my dad would have married Bob if he could have back then, but I know that he believed that this choice should be available to all individuals and that civil rights extends to us all. He would fight hard for that right today even if he did not exercise that choice. Sitcoms today make our family normal. We believe we have been normal for well over fifty years. Thank you Dad and Mom for giving us a stable family environment filled with love, laughter, show tunes, and high heels that make your legs look fabulous.

IF I WERE A KING

Carlos Ziálcita

It was the spring of 1972. I had just come off the road with the LA-based Chico David Blues Band as their harmonica player. It was good to be back in San Francisco, the city where I arrived from Manila in 1958 at the age of 10. After graduating from high school and completing a couple of years at the University of San Francisco, I had lived in Marin County, Los Angeles and briefly in New York City. I was now living in the inner Mission District, a largely working-class Latino neighborhood. Greeted upon my arrival by cherry blossoms in bloom on Guerrero Street and palm trees in Dolores Park, I embraced this new chapter in my young and restless life.

After a strict musical diet of blues and jazz favorites, I was back in the old neighborhood hearing familiar sounds like Marvin Gaye's "What's Goin' On," Al Green's "I'm So Tired Of Being Alone," and "All Day Music" by War. I was a fan of both Santana and Malo, the originators of Latin Rock. In addition, I was introduced by my friends to albums by several New York Latin recording artists including *La Perfecta* by Eddie Palmieri, *Crime Pays* by Willie Colon, and *St. Latin's Day Massacre* by Joe Bataan. Joe's music really appealed to me, mostly because he sang in English, but also because he blended Latin music with Rhythm and Blues.

The music of Joe Bataan filled our living room, where LP covers lay scattered on the floor and leaning against a cinder block bookshelf that housed a turntable. That record player spun non-stop with our favorite music and artists. We were young, energized by the political awareness and cultural celebrations of the time, and always ready for a party. *St. Valentine's Day*

Carlos Ziálcita

Massacre quickly became one of my favorite LPs with the cool cover and great songs like "*Para Puerto Rico Voy*," "Coco-E," "Shaft," "I Wish You Love–Parts 1&2," and "If I Were A King." The rich blend of Rhythm & Blues with what was becoming known at the time as "Salsa" really got to me. Everybody's favorite was "I Wish You Love–Parts 1 & 2" with the great transition of tempo from a Latin Soul love ballad to a smokin' hot dance number. "If I Were A King" especially spoke to me with the soothing doo wop harmonies, the classically hip R&B bass vocal parts, and Joe Bataan pouring his heart out with lyrics that cried...

> *If you say you love me*
> *I'll give you diamonds and furs*
> *Just whisper that you want me*
> *And you'll be my girl*

It was summer and I was invited to a pig roast at a friend's house where I ran into Myrna, a gorgeous, sexy, and vivacious, young Afro-Mayan-Honduran lady I had met before when she and her sister came over to visit my roommate. This is where Myrna and I came together and immediately fell in love. We started dating and soon she moved into my flat on 23rd and Shotwell, where the party rarely stopped and Joe Bataan's music was part of the soundtrack to what became a life-long romance with the love of my life. Again, Joe Battan's lyrics came through:

> *Darling there's gonna be no road long enough*
>   *in the whole wide world*
> *That's gonna stop this guy from walking*
> *And getting to you*
> *There's gonna be no river deep enough baby*
> *That I can't swim to be beside you*

Carlos Ziálcita

If I were a King....If I were a King....

In 1975, Joe Bataan released *Ordinary Guy (Afro-Filipino)* declaring to the world his ethnic roots. I was surprised, thinking as most people probably did that being from East Harlem, he was probably Puerto Rican. "How could he not be Puerto Rican," I thought, thinking back to the songs on Joe's albums: "*Para Puerto Rico Voy,*" "*Es Tu Cosa,*" "*Mujer,*" and "*Coco-e.*" Everyone in the neighborhood loved these songs and thought of Joe as one of our heroes.

Born Bataan Nitollano in 1942 to a Filipino father and an African American mother, Joe grew up in Spanish Harlem, the "East Side" of Harlem in New York City. A singer, songwriter and record producer with numerous hit songs and records, Joe Bataan was one of the original artists of Fania Records. Internationally recognized, the legendary artist brought people and cultures together through music. "My father was Filipino, my mother was African American, and my culture was Puerto Rican," Joe has said.

In the mid-seventies, Joe Bataan, the "King of Latin Soul," was at the peak of his career. Joe described this New York music genre this way: "Latin soul comes straight from the streets of Harlem. It's a cha-cha backbeat with English lyrics and a pulsating rhythm that makes your feet come alive." He is also credited with the first rap record to hit the European market in 1979 with "Rap-O-Clap-O." While it didn't chart domestically, it was a big hit throughout Europe. Soon after this accomplishment, Joe disappeared from the public eye for almost 20 years. He returned to what he knew—his neighborhood. He went back to being a counselor for troubled youth, sharing his experiences and insight. While raising his family, he lived, worked, and served in his community.

In 1995 Joe Bataan returned to the stage and has not stopped since. He resumed his music career and started to tour and record again. His early recordings were still popular with his original fan base, and now Joe Bataan's appeal has crossed over to the Asian, European, Mexican American and South American audiences.

    The San Francisco Filipino American Jazz Festival was founded in 2008 at the SF Main Public Library during a meeting of the Filipino American National Historical Society. I brought up the idea of an annual festival to honor and celebrate Filipino and Filipino American jazz artists. Myrna and I, together with a group of like-minded spirits have been working to fulfill that mission ever since. We first met Joe Bataan and his wife Yvonne at a Northern California concert in 2010 where he was the featured artist. Already intrigued with the idea to present him as part of the Festival, Myrna urged me to get tickets. Joe's riveting performance that night, coupled with his charismatic charm, was a winning combination and served as the impetus to further develop Myrna's original vision. We both wanted to present Joe as a *Balikbayan* artist–returning to his roots as the "Afro-Filipino King of Latin Soul." Although he had recorded *Ordinary Guy (Afro Filipino)* on Salsoul Records back in 1975, Joe didn't enjoy much success with the Filipino American audience and community. Wondering why, Joe himself said "I recorded *Afro-Filipino* back in 1975, what's taking my people so long?"

    In June 2011 the San Francisco Filipino American Jazz Festival presented Joe Bataan in concert, hoping that his 1970s hit *Ordinary Guy (Afro-Filipino)* would resonate with the diverse Bay Area audience. It was a huge success, with a "meet and greet" at the Bayanihan Center in San Francisco, a TV interview on ABS-CBN International–The Filipino Channel, and two sold-out shows at Yoshi's San Francisco in the Fillmore District, a neighborhood once home to many Filipinos. It was a giant multicultural celebration, a homecoming for a Black Pinoy from East Harlem making a connection with his Filipino roots for the first time in the SF Bay Area as a result of this presentation by the San Francisco Filipino American Jazz Festival. For added support, his long-time fans from the New York/Puerto-Rican and the East LA/ South

Bay Mexican American communities were also "in the house." With an all-star band, Joe gave a stellar performance to a standing-room-only audience.

That magical night led to a trip to the Philippines, where Joe was a featured artist at the 2012 Malasimbo Music Festival in Puerto Galera, Mindoro. This was the first time he visited his father's homeland. Like many of the early Filipino immigrants to the United States, his father was never able to return home. Joe fulfilled his own father's dream with this momentous journey. After performing in Australia at the Sydney International Salsa Festival in October 2012, Joe returned to the SF Bay Area to be one of the featured artists of the 5th Annual San Francisco Filipino American Jazz Festival.

> "From New York City, ladies and gentlemen, the Afro-Filipino King of Latin Soul—Joe Bataan!"

It's October 13, 2012 at Yoshi's Jazz Club in Oakland, California, and the name Joe Bataan still resonates with the OG's—the "original gangsters" from the old neighborhood—as well as with younger Salsa enthusiasts who came to dance.

Joe Bataan's concert at Yoshi's Oakland was a special night in many ways. For starters, Joe delivered an incredible performance featuring a killer band and his wife Yvonne as one of the background singers. In addition, at the end of the second sold-out show, I was honored to present Joe with a Lifetime Achievement Award from the Festival in recognition of his many achievements in music and his inspiring work in the community.

All year long, Yoshi's had been celebrating its 40th Anniversary as a jazz club, with signs and T-shirts everywhere on display. Coincidentally, Myrna and I were also celebrating our 40th year together as a couple. This, plus the concert featuring Joe Bataan, whose music we discovered also forty years ago, was what really made this a "night to remember." My *Latina Garifuna Lady* and I caught each other's eye as we smiled and savored the moment.

Carlos Ziálcita

We knew. In our hearts, we felt exactly how special this evening was. We were back in *la Mission*–falling in love and dancing and partying with our friends to the music of Joe Bataan. I closed my eyes for a moment and felt the warm summer breeze of the nights on 23rd and Shotwell with the windows wide open and the music blastin'…

"*If I were a King…. If I were a King…*"

Portions of "If I Were a King" by Carlos Ziálcita first appeared in the January 15, 2013 issue of *Positively Filipino* magazine: "Joe Bataan: Ordinary Guy With An Extraordinary Heart."
Lyrics from "If I Were A King" by Joe Bataan is used with permission from the artist.

Cultural Bridges

LETTER TO MY KADKADUA

Jeffrey Tangonan Acido

Mag-anka Jeffrey Dalere Tangonan, my kadkadua:

Agmurmurayka! Breathe the air of your ancestors.

Now you see, now you see: You are not an accident of life. Your mother meant it all, this fact of your birthing, its substance and what it means to her and to you. The facts are wrought in stone, those hardy excess of the mountains and hills that depress into the *lukong* of your birthday, until that *lukong*—indeed, the Ilocos—reaches out to the vast sea in the west: born July 3, 1985, in the days of disquiet of your birth land, some few months before the people would rise up in revolution against the dictator with only their rage to call the shots so he, the dictator, would remember, that he had not the right to stay a second longer in power. So you were a prelude to the newfound birth of people's courage, mind you. You never knew—but now you do.

Like everyone else in your barrio, you were born away from the loneliness of hospitals or clinics. You were with your people, in the very heart of it all: in the warm and smoky kitchen built by your grandfather who had come to Hawaii to seek his fortune over here, maybe misfortune, but fortune nonetheless.

I could imagine the welcome, my dear *kadkadua*: our twin cries breaking the silence in that hour of our birth, pacifying the anxiety, and giving calm and balm to the mother of our child's dreams, in the Philippines and in Hawaii, much later on. Our whole neighborhood could have come to give witness to this birthing, the midwife with her crude but certain ways, and the relatives' prayers that went with their frenzied ways of attending to the needs of both mother and midwife—and then us.

Someone could have gathered the leaves: the *marunggay* to coax our mother's breast so she would have more colostrum, the first of the first milk we would need.

Someone could have put out the *basi*, the *arak*, the tobacco, the gaiety could have begun right there and then, despite our young father's absence.

You see: he had to go away to fight a war he did not understand. Perhaps he did not like to wage a war with others, but Ilocos being Ilocos, with its parched earth and broken promises, he did not have to justify his leaving, for leaving he had to fight a war for a dictator who bluffed his way into greatness as empty as the fields lying fallow when the first rains of May fail us.

So we were born without him, coming into this world in war and in chaos, and in the din of what was left of the Philippines in those times with rallies and demonstrations that marked each day that we had to fight it out, with mother finally deciding to let go of the homeland and join her family over here so we could have a chance, one fat chance to be something better, to eke it out somewhere else in the hope that in eking out, some life would come to us at last.

And so we left, you remember that. We left the barrio of our birth to get into another barrio—the same poverty we were escaping from—in the big city, where soldiers like our father were doomed to be poor, where the poor were doomed to be poorer.

In the big city, we waited for the coming of our younger sister, Des. Des, who had come with smiles on her face, sunny smiles, bright smiles, and whose charm gave some hope for a land so rendered hopeless.

With us, you my *kadkadua*, Des, and I, we waited for our parents to come home, our mother from a faraway land she had gone to, and our father from the many wars he had to fight in Mindanao.

Some days, our mother would come, but not long—and Des would not know her, remember? Perhaps I was more understanding, more tolerant of absences? Perhaps I was getting used to it, this life with our neighbors shared day in day out, a life of absence, a life of constant looking for something better, something more redeeming beyond the small piece of meat we would share with equally poor children?

Kadkadua: You realize at a very early age that in the geography of pain and separation your neighbors were closer to you than your family in Hawaii—both in reach and intimacy. And your birthland is the same thing, despite its wretchedness: it is where you wanted to stay longer—and linger on. You remember the ceremonies of arriving and departing from this birthland, the ceremonies in the language you knew: Ilokano. Some night an adult with you tagging along would take the bus, and in the morning sunlight, there you were in Bacarra, in those flat lands of rice and garlic that in the east would reach up to the mountains and in the west would bow to the power of the waters of the sea.

This land of the Ilokos you returned to many times, as if in a ritual. And when it was time for you to leave, you just called out to your name: *Umaykan, umaykan, di ka agbatbati!* (Come, come, you are not to be left behind!) Of course, you were calling out to yourself.

I was calling out to you, my *kadkadua*.

The sounds of your first language, you are sure, are the powerful winds of the Ilokos mountains, the clatter of the water buffalo's steps as it pulls the sled that carries the *bolo* knives and shovels that allow the earth to breathe, and the flow of the water of life to the thirsty rice fields of the Ilokos. Do not allow this language to be dead in you, *kadkadua*. It will be a struggle, yes, but it will be your connection to the gods and goddesses you will search for. There is no shortcut to the redeeming ways of the gods and the goddesses, you see.

- *kadkadua:* Ilokano word for placenta, twin, companion, to journey with, spirit, soul
- *agmurmuray:* to shake off drowsiness shortly after waking up to become completely awake
- *arak:* wine
- *basi:* fermented sugarcane
- *lukong:* lowlands, flatlands
- *marunggay:* horse-radish tree (*Moringa oleifera*)

"HAUNTED"

Jeannie Barroca

Ours was an insular, haunted adolescence, one of a handful of Filipino families in the Midwest.

We heard cryptic references to the *aswang*, the Filipino version of the worst bogey-person designed to keep children near to the hearth and away from strangers. The circuitous *aswang* version that we finally heard, after many interruptions on our part, seemed to linger too long on girls having babies at all:

Mom: *Aswang will sit on the roof till everyone's asleep. Then she sticks her long tongue down into the house and steals the baby from the mother (pause) don't get pregnant...*

Us: *On the roof like where you lived? Aswang would fall through...*

Us: *What's pregnant?*

Mom: *Only her tongue gets into the house. She's still on the roof. Men get you a baby inside you. So once aswang gets the baby, it will grow up to be aswang, too...*

Us: *Is the tongue coiled up in her head?*

Us: *How does the men get babies inside?*

Mom: *And sometimes she flies. You're too young, I'll tell you later. There's a book I can show you. Aswang's tongue can go anywhere. Just don't play with boys. And don't sit on your uncle's lap anymore.*

This is how we alternately heard about both spooky stuff and stuff "down there."

Jeannie Barroga

For us six-and-seven year olds, my brother, Kenny, and myself, the real psychic discovery was telepathy: he was the sender, and I was the receiver. Even our close births played a part: Kenny's less than eleven months younger. For forty days every year, he and I are technically the same age. Somehow with our combined senses, we'd hear the knocks, voices, find lost objects, see the mists, and smell aromas. Plus, we could both draw. We could verify each of our dreams or visions. Oh, the book mom mentioned? It covered menstrual periods. Mom said specifically to me, don't draw this. Somehow even back then, no one could tell me what not to write. Unlike Kenny, I kept minute details. Recalling details determined back then how I now write.

Minnie was the former owner of our house, an old, sickly woman who actually died in the attic bedroom. A constant, wispy presence once Kenny moved to that roof-slanted area.

The epitome of sightings was of Minnie, like a skipped record, her appearance played continuously on moonlit nights. She would float forward three feet, appear behind herself, and float forward again. I dived between my bed and Kenny's timing it for me to make it just as Minnie was the farthest away. I miscalculated. I could see her white image at my elbow so I closed my eyes and dived. Kenny just laughed; he was used to Minnie.

I don't think these psychic "gifts" were passed on by Dad, who regaled us with his story of the dead priest's ghostly footsteps outside Ormoc City's bombed church during WWII. But it was easy to dismiss Dad's encounter: he was a mischievous, drunk soldier. Mom? Well, she seemed absolutely clueless whenever our cries in the night about closet ghosts brought her into our four-child bedroom. Dad hit the sack early working six days a week and never heard our cries. He'd awe us with the ghost priest but dismissed our own renditions of ghosts, right there in our own house. As I seemed to be the "sensitive" one, Mom would respond mostly to my nightly calls. She'd then sleep in late, staying up long hours till we were calmed down before taking her own rest. Was it only Filipino households where there was so much left unsaid? Psychically, parts of our house were more active than others.

In a recent adult moment, Ken and I watched as Mom maneuvered out the door into the afternoon sun. A swirl of odd orbs gathered, halted around her and, just as the door closed behind her, were sucked out into the sunlight that backlit her, stuck to her. Ken turned to me and asked, "Do you remember the night of the lights?"

The image swirled back in my memory: pretty lights, like Tinkerbell, had floated out of the closet, dancing on the ceiling; we kids coo and aw. The lights become bigger, brighter, faster. They swoop now, clipping me in the upper bunk and diving down and away from Kenny. Our oohs become barks of surprise, then fear, then screams of terror. The whole room is one massive sweep of menacing lights till Mom opens the door to darkness, no lights, except from the spill from the TV room. We're whimpering, but she is impatient, tired of this almost daily nocturnal routine of fears and spectres.

It struck me then: Mom was, emotionally, the catalyst, all along. Spirits, and old dreams, and terrors stuck to her, roamed the house, and then, with no place to go, they stuck to us. I told her about the orbs we saw and then asked, "Mom, you never believed us, all those nights. How could you not have anything happen to you?" Her answer: "I didn't want to scare you. I've been seeing things all my life."

Another adult revelation: she knew! She continued, "In Ormoc City, I'd say nothing as a child. Day or night I'd hear voices, noises. At night in that house, it was like a party, after you kids finally went to sleep. I didn't sleep much till morning."

We hardly ever saw Mom when we went off to school. I never thought of her late nights watching TV was her standing guard for the house. The psychic connection is from HER line. The fears and dealing with all of them, HER methods.

Jeannie Barroga

    Only a full book could detail all the happenings in that house. Mom's undisclosed admission and desire to not scare us obviously didn't work. Us siblings are aware of all the spirits hanging on. We all are intrigued to this day about things unexplained and paranormal. Ours is a guarded legacy: our silence is a palpable spirit in itself.

TRIBUTE TO OSCAR

Evangeline Canonizado Buell

*I*n 2009, Oscar Peñaranda, professor and community leader, led a group of fourteen Filipino Americans—some from the Filipino American National Historical Society (FANHS) and others from the community-at-large—to the Philippines for a one-month tour of Luzon to Mindanao. Some of us were going for the first time or returning for the second or third time. Many of us wanted to reunite with relatives or find our ancestors to discover and learn about our roots. Before leaving for the Philippines, Oscar did a lot of research to locate our relatives by contacting churches, schools, friends, and teachers, etc. He was diligent in making the contacts so that our trip would be fruitful in finding our connection to long-lost or undiscovered relatives.

I wanted to find at least one cousin, however distant, and I knew there were many Canonizado's in San Antonio, Zambales. Oscar had checked it out, and we connected with his contact—a principal of a school in Subic Bay who led us to San Antonio to a cousin who would be there to greet us.

Oscar (our leader), a guide, a driver, and my 24-year-old granddaughter, Brielle, set out together. Upon arrival we met with the county clerk, a Canonizado by marriage who was to help us locate the cousin. It turned out she was not there and had taken off on a vacation. Our clerk said, "Don't worry, we'll go back to the courthouse and look up other Canonizado's to see if they may be available to meet you." She went through the files, came back to us, and asked, "Is your father's correct name Estanislao Canonizado?" and I excitedly said yes. She responded by saying, "You have a sister here, your father's daughter!" I was totally shocked—I remember my dad showing me a picture of her when I was a little girl. He told me she was my half sister. He had been married to another woman before he left the Philippines to join the American Navy in 1917. I had no idea she would be alive as she, I know, was considerably older than I, and I had not heard about her since my dad died in 1957. It never occurred to me to ask about her.

The police were requested to lead our group to her home. The court house clerk had called in advance to let them know we were coming.

As we walked into her home, we were greeted by her sons and care givers who wheeled her out in a wheel chair to meet us. I broke into tears, as did she and the entire party: police, our driver, guide, the county clerk, Brielle, Oscar. All of us wept tears of joy.

And I, in shock and in disbelief saying to myself, I have a half sister—a relative, my father's daughter. I handed her my father's photographs and she hugged them to her heart. I glanced over to Oscar, and there were tears in his eyes, and I was overwhelmed with joy!

I thank Oscar for reuniting me with my long-lost sister. She died just before Christmas 2012. I was fortunate to meet her and it was because of Oscar's great warmth, compassion, and love for people that made this happen to me and others on the trip who were reunited with long-lost and undiscovered relatives. I now stay in touch with my sister Rosalina's daughter, Rosemarie Puquiz. As a Filipino American born, I will now always be a part of the Philippines. I have family there.

BIRTH TO THE ANCIENT IN NEW TIME
Tess Crescini

A hand beckons towards the forest of my dreams—
A vendor pushing a cart watching the dancers,
The drummers pulsating, calling the ancestors
like a yearning deeper than the sea.
The sacred history whispers itself back.
The silence of my soul listens, waits
for ancestral memory in this dream landscape
to give birth to the ancient in new time.

A *malong*, a tubular cloth from the Maranao tribe
Of Southern Philippines, imprints its story through
Patterns their hands have known before birth,
Used to wrap a new born baby,
To carry a child while walking, working
Worn by both men and women,
Laid down as a prayer mat,
as a cover for the body during sleep,
or naps on lazy afternoons tied between trees as a hammock,
As shade from the sun,
As protection for the head while carrying baskets of wares to sell
                                                          in the public market,
As a wrap for the body about to be buried or burned to ashes—

The way of my ancestors, the ones who read the stars
To navigate across the blue oceans and emerald green islands.

Tess Crescini

The conch shell blows echoes, bounces on the mountains
And takes flight with the breeze, calling me to come home
Like the waves that rush to shore,
The dreamer awakens,
Declares this is my medicine,
The way of my ancestors.

DOMINADOR CRUZ MANUEL

Brenda Manuel Fulton

I remember waking to hear awful sounds coming from my mother like I had never heard before. I walked into the big bathroom to see my father lying on the floor with his eyes closed. He was lying very still while my mother cradled him and cried out loudly. I saw her face all twisted in pain when she looked up at us standing in the doorway. It scared me to see her like this. My older sister, Linda, shifted us into the next room and told us to keep quiet and get dressed by ourselves. Then she said, "Daddy's dead."

The next thing I knew, our house was filled with many people. Aunts, uncles and many of my father's friends that spoke Tagalog. I often hid and sat underneath the dining room table when my father's friends came to visit. He would offer them whiskey in a pretty glass. They would begin to talk in words with high and low pitches that I could not understand. My father would often leave the room and come back with money. He would pass this quickly to their hands before they left. I could see all since I was underneath the table.

My three sisters and I, and my five brothers were all moved from the bedroom to the toy room. The curtains were quickly drawn. The television and the mirrors in the house were covered with sheets. I asked my auntie, "Why?" I was told not to ask questions and to speak softly and whisper, otherwise the spirits would capture my soul and take me too. I tiptoed around and whispered from that moment on. I was seven years old. After waiting quietly for a short time, we were lined up and taken into my father's room. My aunts, uncles and friends were crowded around the bed that my father was lying on.

My father's room was filled with people. Everybody was crying. There was a priest on the other end of the bed holding an open bible and speaking in Latin while he sprinkled my father with holy water. My mother was on the side of the priest, sobbing quietly now. When she saw us enter the room, she came to us and told us to kiss our father and this would be the last time we'd ever see him again.

I was scared of everything. I did not want to kiss my father. I wanted out of this crowded room. I wanted to sit at the kitchen table again and dunk white bread in my father's creamed, sweet coffee and look at him, smiling across the table before he left to work. I wanted to be with him while he watched boxing while we'd run around his leather chair and took turns sliding over his shoulders and slipping down his two legs. I wanted to hear him play, "Never On A Sunday," on his saxophone once more. I wanted to help him place his gold, shiny saxophone inside that dark purple, softly lined, velvet saxophone case.

I often sat outside in the hallway and peeked in the doorway of this same bedroom. I'd watch my father play his saxophone for hours and listen to beautiful sounds from his saxophone. Sheets of music he had written in blue ink were scattered all around the floor.

Now he lay there in front of this crowd with his eyes closed and stiff and lifeless for everyone to stare at. I wanted them out of my father's room. They were not allowed to be here in his special room for music. I wanted to escape away from all these strangers and felt sickened by the priest dressed in black and white and everyone crying loudly. I looked behind me for a way out from under all the elbows, but when I quickly turned towards the door and found a path, my aunt grabbed my arm and pushed me towards my father's face. She shoved my neck down and said, "Kiss him." My face was pushed against his cold skin and I reluctantly kissed his cold, cold cheek. After, we were taken to the dark toy room again and told to be quiet.

We were not allowed to go to my father's funeral. My grandmother told us that there were evil spirits in the graveyards that came out of their graves and took little children's souls. But all my cousins had gone to my father's funeral and I felt so cheated that we were not allowed to go.

My grandmother came and stayed with us after my father had died. The only time I remember seeing my mother is when I could hear her crying loudly. She would lock herself in the little bathroom and cry for hours. My uncles would have to come and unscrew the screws from the doorway jams in order to remove the door from the bathroom. Then they would carry my mother off the floor as she wept, and the doctor would come to the house to give her a shot. I would catch a glimpse of her face when they lifted her. Her long, beautiful, black, wavy hair was matted to her cheek, wet from her tears being pressed against the floor. Her soft, white skin was streaked red from crying. She was only 28. Her eyes, floating and searching, looked lost somewhere within our large house. I'd try to touch her, to grab hold of her hand to feel comfort but my uncles and grandmother would push me back and say, "Your mother is sick right now. Do not touch her or bother her."

I played outdoors during that time and took care of my younger sister, Tina. Tina and I climbed up high on the tractor to play, or we'd play house in the empty chicken coops. Sometimes we would collect pinecones from our large pine tree or play dolls with our Skipper and Barbie. We played tag. We collected small, white eucalyptus seeds from our eucalyptus trees. We played jump rope. We gathered dead birds we found on the property from the insecticides they sprayed on the strawberry and artichoke fields nearby. We'd bury them and make little crosses from sticks we found to put on their graves.

When it got dark outside, we came into the kitchen and ate my grandmother's fresh, homemade tortillas and refried beans. It was so silent in our house and all the mirrors were covered in dark fabric and the curtains remained closed.

But when I entered the bedroom that I shared with my sisters, Linda,

Sandra and Tina, a different world was happening. I opened the door of our bedroom to hear my oldest sister, Linda, singing with the radio. The curtains were opened. The windows were opened. There were posters pinned up on the walls of television stars I recognized: Dr. Kildare, Ben Casey, Ozzie and Harriet's son and the Rifleman. My sister was chewing gum. She stood in front of the mirror ratting her hair in a high mess above her hairline. Her lips were painted a frosted pink and she had drawn dark lines above her eyelids. I had never seen her look like this before. She would soon be fourteen.

My grandmother left after six months. My mother cut off her long, black hair that was down to her waist. She worked days and evenings in the packing sheds, sorting and packing carrots or whatever vegetable was in season to pay the taxes on our land and provide for us children. The animals were sold; the barn and chicken coops knocked down and two apartments went up instead. We had a myriad of teenage babysitters during this time. My two older sisters took on many responsibilities. Linda took over cooking and making all our dresses for school. Sandra took care of feeding my three baby brothers, 2-year-old Dexter, 1-year-old Darol, and David Dean who was only 27 days old when my father passed away. The rest of us children took care of the one youngest to us in age and learned to watch over them.

After losing my father, we lost all contact with many of my father's Filipino friends. They stopped inviting us over for the celebrations we were used to having. Our uncles, aunties and cousins that had come over often, suddenly disappeared. I realized then that these "uncles, aunties and cousins" were never my real family because they did not care for us now.

We struggled along for two years without my father until my mother had her boyfriend live with us. He was a German immigrant man that eventually became my stepfather. The fish and rice dishes we had daily were suddenly gone and replaced with potatoes, sausage, sauerkraut and stinky cheese.

Brenda Manuel Fulton

An uncomfortable feeling existed in our home now with strict rules from this strange German man that came in to replace our father. We lost everything we had ever known about being Filipino, the day my father passed away.

FILIPINO WEDDINGS
Brenda Manuel Fulton

We went to many weddings when I was a child, not just any wedding but Filipino weddings. Every Filipino family in our community came out for this special event and dressed up in their best clothes.

The excitement of the wedding was in the preparation and killing of the pig for the wedding feast. A fat, good-looking pig was chosen and held in our barn until the day of the wedding.

Many of my father's friends came by to see the pig and gleam over how grand it was and to discuss what a well-chosen animal it would make for the feast. Others dropped by our home to look at the pig in the backyard and to discuss who should kill it. I often thought more attention went into the choosing and killing of the pig than in any other part of the wedding since it generated much excitement in our family and among Filipino friends.

The day before the wedding was the celebratory day that the pig was slaughtered. Carloads of my father's friends came for the event. They were all brown-skinned, small-framed Filipino men with flat noses and big warm smiles. This was a big day. This was tradition.

The oldest, most experienced man, Uncle Pete, was chosen to kill the pig. Uncle Pete arrived very early in the morning before the others. He dug a pit in the ground and threw dried, broken twigs from our trees in the ground. He started the fire. A large, thick, blackened and worn, square grill was placed over the pit and the fire started to crackle and grow. Two huge metal pots were placed over the grill with water to boil.

Several men arrived and carried the long picnic table over by the pit. They covered the table with plastic cloth and set out big bowls and sharp knives. Killing a pig stirred up more enthusiasm and excitement between the men in the Filipino community than anything else, well, maybe other than a rooster fight.

There were at least fifty or more men that gathered around talking, smoking and drinking in the early morning sun and discussing that pig. But Uncle Pete was the focus of attention. He would have the grand honor of killing the pig.

Men arrived and looked for Uncle Pete to shake his hand. He was the chosen one—the smallest of all the men with his knees bent slightly when walking and a slight hunch when he walked. When he smiled, all his crooked teeth could not take away the warmth he gave you. There was much laughter and joking when the groom arrived to witness the killing and the group of men became larger, as more and more Filipino men arrived to witness this grand tradition.

I watched from my bedroom window as the pig was let out and tied to the tree. My brothers were allowed to participate in these events, but I was not since I was a girl. When the fire was very hot and the water was boiling, the pig was untied and let loose in the center of the crowd. The pig would squeal and run around and the men laughed, dodging the running pig. Clouds of dirt blew up from the scuffling of shoes and from the pig running everywhere. The men still remained in a large circle surrounding the pig in the center. The men laughed and laughed until Uncle Pete wrestled the pig down and laid the pig on its side and tied the pig's legs tightly together with rope. Then I could see the men lift and carry the pig onto the long, picnic table covered with plastic. They laid the pig on top of the table, on its side.

All the men gathered closely around the table and it grew very silent. I could no longer see what was taking place from my window, but I could see the steam from the pots of boiling water going up into the air.

I always knew when the pig was actually killed. There was a dead silence, no more laughter or the shuffling of feet or laughter. No man moved his body. Then I listened quietly for what was to happen next when I suddenly heard one last, loud, crying squeal echo out in the air and I knew it was over. The men quieted down after this and there was no more laughter. The men gathered in small groups to smoke and drink. Then I saw one man go to the side of the table where the pig laid on its side carrying a very wide pot. He stood where the pig was and bent over, close to the pig, to collect the dripping blood from where the pig's neck had been slit open.

Several men gathered around the picnic. They worked busily at the table. Their rubber boots were splattered with the pig's blood. The men quieted down after the slaughter. Many helped cook the meat and take it into the kitchen to make blood meat, roast pork and pork *adobo*. Some of the men left. Others stayed around talking, smoking, pouring Uncle Pete a Crown Royal whiskey and drank along with him while finishing the work of cutting up the pig and cooking it.

The wedding took place the next day at our Catholic church, Madonna del Sasso. The service was very long and boring with the priest speaking in Latin, which nobody understood. I only remembered to pound on my heart three times when the bell rang out and to stand and kneel at the appropriate times and also, to remember to make the sign of the cross often. I wanted it to be over so I could eat roast pig.

Finally after the church service we crowded in line, waiting for the bride and groom to enter so we could eat the food, which was the best part of the wedding. Roast pig, blood meat, pork *adobo*, *pansit* noodles, rice and sweet, deep fried coconut balls. I don't remember the wedding cake, but I remember all the other wonderful things I ate that day.

Then came the money dance. I was even allowed at my young age to dance with the groom. My mother gave me money to pin on the groom and said I must dance with him because it was very good luck for me.

When Uncle Pete arrived, he was given as much attention as the bride and everyone clapped. People stood up, smiled at him and took time to talk to him. Some shook his hand and hugged him and brought him a drink. He smiled and held a cigar in his other hand. Uncle Pete was a very special man on this day.

I discovered as a child that the slaughtering of the pig was the most important part of every Filipino wedding because it brought everyone in the community together to share in this very special tradition. This was the way it had always been done in the Philippines.

THE RAID

Herb Jamero

"Boy, tell the truth now. You can trust me. Was there a rooster fight here today?" Questions came from a tall uniformed officer from the County Sheriff's Department shortly after descending at my *campo* home on a rare raid for the *Sabong*, an illegal rooster fight. How to answer knowing I was being watched not only by an officer of the law but my father as well as the other *manongs*. I felt cornered and conflicted. Yes. I knew it was illegal as well as bloody and brutal but also a significant social and cultural event within the Filipino culture. I flashed to another day, about a year earlier, when I witnessed my father paying off the local Chief of Police from my hiding place. I was then to learn later that this was how these rooster fights were allowed to continue. Historically, this practice met with the tacit permission of the townspeople who preferred that Filipinos not gather in town. This was the town whose own Assemblyman introduced the resolution that "Filipinos were Undesirable." Congress then eventually changed the legal status of Filipinos from "national" to "alien." Concurrently, anti-miscegenation laws were passed that prohibited Filipinos from marrying Whites as well as property laws denying further rights. Anti-Filipino riots were still raw with bitter memories. Against this backdrop, my first personal awareness of a cultural conflict was experienced.

It was a typical, hot, summer Sunday, the day in the week that everyone looked forward to for a variety of reasons. For truly, Sunday is for *Sabong*. Our labor camp housed from eighty to a hundred Pinoys from a generation-of immigrants recruited from the rural areas of the Philippines to provide a labor force for the plantations, fields, orchards and canneries of America. Backbreaking work. Stoop labor. Tired to the bone and aching muscles. Caked with a mixture of dirt and sweat. Looking forward to a day of rest and recreation. What better than that day of rest proclaimed by Christians everywhere—Sunday! Sunday was not only a day of rest from a long week of 10-hour work days but to relax, reminisce with *kababayans*, and to indulge in their cultural pastime—the Sunday cockfight.

These were men tied to their work and shackled by an intolerant society. For these men, this was a time to channel their pent-up energy into a favorite event and to literally "let loose." This was what they were looking for throughout their long workweek. This meant more than just a sporting event. They were as one with these fighting cocks. This could be seen in the manner in which they groomed then preened themselves—the way they often strutted on the sidewalks of California's cities dressed in their double-breasted gabardine suits and in their combative stance as they sought a better life for themselves. After all, these were the same trailblazers who had fought bitterly and died defending their rights, first in Hawaii's plantations, then in the dusty fields of California.

For the owners of these fighting cocks, this was the time when their coddling and training skills came to a test. Roosters bred for the sole purpose of pitting one against the other to the death. Beautiful birds whose feathers reflected a blend of colors from brilliant scarlets and whites to softer hues of oranges and yellows to vivid blacks, yet menacing in the way they strutted and fluffed their feathers to show their fearlessness and natural aggressiveness. With sharp knives strapped to spurs, a deadly fighting machine emerged. When loosed and neck feathers fluffed, they would fly at each other with their razor-sharp knives poised to maim and kill until one fell in defeat. For the encircling audience, there was a shared sense of excitement and electricity.

The air itself was filled with a mix of roars of approval for the fighting skills of these roosters, followed by victorious shouts by the winners and moans of dismay by the losers. For the many spectators, as well as the owners, there was an opportunity to gamble and bet their hard-earned money on this illegal event.

This was a day for families as well. We were scattered throughout the surrounding countryside and Sunday was a day for the children to socialize, play different games, test our shooting skills on a Daisy BB gun, flirt with the girls, and hang around with our "uncles" for handouts and to run errands if needed. For the mothers, a Sunday was not only a reprieve from their own duties as mother and homemaker but also the task of working alongside their husbands on their family farm when time permitted. For these same mothers, this was an opportunity to improve their economic station by making then selling mouth-watering delicacies. Each seemed to have her own ethnic specialty. Manang "Ika" for her *biko*. Manang "Toria" for her *bitso bitso*. Manang Alepia for her *maruya* and *bibingka*. Mama for her *binangkal*. Señoras Juanita and Frances for their Mexican dishes. And Mary for her fried chicken. For everyone, a festive day indeed.

In the midst of all this activity, the dreaded phone call from our local police chief who warned my father of a pending raid from the County Sheriff. This phone call was in exchange for the payoff arrangement that we would be notified should a raid be planned. In any event, as if rehearsed, the following took place. The out-of-towners tucked their roosters in their homemade cages and left the immediate area by the back roads. The men of the camp returned their own roosters to their cages located adjacent to the bunkhouse and hid all the paraphernalia associated with fighting roosters, especially the knives. The mothers bid their children around them and their food stalls. In the meantime, a group of men gathered chairs and benches in a crude semi-circle simulating a socializing, visiting area. While this was going on, *manongs* and uncles collected their own personal musical string instruments. Uncle Carnuto with his prized Gibson guitar. Manong Pascual with his homemade washtub bass. Another *manong* with his mandolin. And other guitar players that soon there was an impromptu string band that could play both traditional folk songs as well as assorted popular hits of the day. In front of this band, a cleared area was made for dancing. Even now, I can hear the faint strains of songs such as "You'll Never Know" and "Slow Boat To China." Also, a favorite of the *manongs* and the Mexican ladies: "Mexicali Rose" with all its longing and yearning of a long-lost love. Amazingly, within a relatively short time, an area transformed from a cock-fighting venue to a party took form.

Then, almost on time, a small procession of official county cars began to descend then surround our property. Surprisingly and somewhat disappointing at least to me, no sounds of sirens. Uniformed officers then emerged with the spokesman requesting to speak to my father. After a few moments of polite but confrontational conversation, a search then took place. Confiscated were several cages with roosters and fighting paraphernalia left behind or forgotten by the out-of-towners in their haste to leave. All this time, the band kept playing almost as a backdrop to the drama taking place. I was transfixed by this drama. It was exciting. It was scary. Everything in slow motion. What would happen next? Then, an unwelcome thought, "What would my *Puti* (White) schoolmates think and say tomorrow?" Pushing my own concerns aside, I returned my focus on my father. I will always remember my father's calmness in speaking with the officer. A leader among the men who sometimes referred to him as "boss." He led by example in this confrontation. A prevailing sense of pride came to me in this revelation of my father who had mostly been a fearful and intimidating father figure. Little did I know that this was to be the beginning of a different and more positive relationship.

"Boy, tell the truth now. You can trust me. Was there a rooster fight here today?" A question seemingly coming out of nowhere from an unknown law

Herb Jamero

officer who had singled me out. How should I answer? Then, with a sense of new felt confidence, my answer: "Sir, it's my brother's birthday, not a rooster fight." While he seemed dubious of my answer, from the corner of my eye I saw "PaPa" give a small nod of approval.

MY LIFE AS A LUMPIA

Jessica A. Jamero

"Jessica Amour Jamero!" I hear the omen of my full name being called as I stop my homework and peek out my bedroom door to where my mom is sitting at the dining room table. The dark oak four-leaf table is the center of my home both physically and socially. The table serves as an open book of memories that spans across my family's history. It is here that my family laughs, cries, celebrates, mourns, and deals with each other's pains. It is also a modern day scaffold where my brother and I sit while being punished alternately by my parents who live in San Jose and Papa (Grandpa Herb), with whom my brother and I have lived since I was in the seventh grade. Judging by the tone of Mom's voice and that I was being summoned by my full name, I think the latter is the case.

I leave my bedroom, seat myself at the opposite end of the table from Mom, and give her a slightly annoyed look. "Ok, what did I do now?" I ask, indifferent to what the answer might be. "You know we are rolling *lumpia* on Saturday and Papa tells me you have plans to see a movie with your friends. Is that true?" Why do parents always ask stupid questions like this? Obviously it's true if Papa said so. "Urn, yeah... the gang and I wanna go to a movie. Is there a problem with that?" Ooops! I should have left that last part out as I now have to avoid her obviously peeved stare. "Yes, there is a problem with that," my mom replies. She drones on about needing my help and that the dining room table can be easily extended to make room for all of us including me— there goes that line of defense. Seeing no other out, I give in to what I know was a no-win situation.

After my failed attempt at getting out of lumpia wrapping, I called my friends to tell them the bad news. My first call was to Leslie who, to my surprise, was not disappointed about canceling our movie plans. "Cool! Can I help?" Leslie said with enthusiasm. I replied, "Leslie, you do not want to come and help. There are going to be old people here talking about back in the good ole days when they had to walk miles to school." I pride myself on mimicking old people. Leslie answered, "Yeah, but Jess, old people are cool. Plus we get lumpia!" Ok, so she has a point. We do get lumpia. My next call was to Luis. "Awesome, we get food!" another enthusiastic betrayal. "Luis, it's just lumpia." I complained to no avail. "Yeah, and we get to eat it. I'll be there!"

The rest of the week passes by in a blur and when Friday night arrives I am grateful for the week to be over. I think of the weekend of rest and relaxation that awaits me when I suddenly see a dark cloud looming over the horizon of my beautiful and lazy weekend. It's the dark shadow of a huge, deep fried and stuffed to the gills lumpia. Being resigned to the fact that my plans for the weekend are shot, I ended up wasting time surfing the internet late into the night until I got tired and retreated into my room.

When I wake up the next morning, I see the light outside. My first goal for the day is accomplished since the sun is set high in the sky which means it's mid-morning and I'm still in bed. A silent scream of joy emerges as the smell of breakfast finds its way to my nose, but I don't smell kielbasa cooking, not the smell of pancakes or French toast. I realize that it's the smell of ground pork, onions and garlic, soy sauce mixed in with bean sprouts, French cut beans, and peas. This is the stuffing of the lumpia and although delectable, it's a reminder that my Saturday will be wasted with lumpia.

I stumble out of bed to start the day and glance back at the clock only to realize it's already 11:30. Papa usually wakes me up promptly at 9:00 saying

I'm "burning daylight." He must be too busy with lumpia preparations to bother with me today. I open my door only to be overwhelmed by the pungent smell of lumpia. Looking out the kitchen window, I see that family members are gathered outside on the porch talking. Before anyone notices I'm awake, I duck back into my room to have "me time" and avoid being asked to do morning chores before my friends arrive.

When Leslie and Luis arrive, we sit at the table with my family. Since my friends have never wrapped lumpia, my *Ninang* (Godmother) and matriarch of the family, Auntie Luna, proceeds to instruct the newcomers in her best impression of a Filipino accent. "Pirst you tik your wrap an put it in pront ob you so dat one point is pacing you. Den you tik some ob de stupping an put in your wrap and pold it ober. Den you pold de udder two corners into de middle an roll tightly. Pretend dat you are rolling a joint an not a burrito!" I gasped, "Ninang! I don't think my friends know how to roll a joint." Everyone around the table laughed at Auntie's attempt at humor and her Filipino accent.

Leslie finished wrapping her first lumpia saying, "I think I sorta know how this goes." Acting as quality inspector, I told her that her corners were too loose; the ends were not moistened so the wrap was not tight enough and it looked more like a burrito than a joint. After making that last comment, all eyes including those of my mom, fixed on me. "Uh, not that I've ever seen a joint or anything. It's just that it is way too big." "Nice save, Jess," Mom says. The group continues to roll; the finished lumpias are being wrapped more tightly and are nearly perfect.

Stories are exchanged by everyone seated around the table. The stories and jokes are all too familiar to me. One of Papa's favorite stories is when he and the Mexican kids in school would trade lunches—he and his siblings, tired of their rice and fish, and their Mexican schoolmates, tired of their tortillas. While the stories continued, I found myself becoming completely absorbed in rolling and trying to get through my pile of wrappers quickly so I could move on with my day. I focus from one wrap to the next not looking around, not taking a break, but becoming one with the lumpia. I even begin to see myself as a lumpia. I see the various ingredients that make lumpia as parallels to my multi-ethnic background. I am Scottish, Irish, German, Chinese and Filipino wrapped in a skin of golden brown similar to the way lumpia looks after it is deep-fried. Mom often expresses her desire for me to know more about her White side of the family and their traditions. I explain to her that I simply connect better with my Filipino side and through no fault of my own. Having been heavily influenced by my Papa, a man steeped in Filipino traditions who enrolled me in folk dance classes and fed me dishes like *adobo* and *pancit* every day during the most impressionable years of my life, it's no wonder.

Suddenly, I am pulled back to reality by an outburst of laughing. I look around and notice that my friends are laughing and generally having a great time with everyone. I look from face to face focusing on the beautifully aged, brown faces and thinning white hair of my elders. My gaze ends with Papa. I find myself looking closely at his plump, brown face and shaggy, white goatee that makes him look like Mr. Miagi from the movie *The Karate Kid*. I look at him intently and try to read between the wrinkles on his face, remembering the stories I have listened to time and time again as he reminisced with his old friends. I sigh with contentment and suddenly realize that I've taken it all for granted. I am so fortunate to have the opportunity to visit with my elders, the people who made my history and to ask questions about their lives to get a better understanding of who they are and where they've been. I realize that the people sitting around the old oak table are those who mean the most to me in the world and those who I mean the most to.

With this realization, I turn to Papa and ask, "How did you and Nana Jeanne meet?" Papa looks at me with an expression of slight bewilderment, then smiles as his eyes sparkle with a hint of a tear as he begins his story.

PAPA'S TWO LEFT FEET

Emily Porcincula Lawsin

We should have known something was seriously wrong when the cops showed up at our front door, asking for my father. The personalized vanity license plates on his sky blue Ford Taurus are what did him in. "Were you driving that car earlier today?" the police officer asked him, pointing to the dented fender of "KaEmang's" car—with a *Santo Niño* on the dash—parked in our driveway. My mother hid behind the hallway banister, shaking her head, realizing for the first time that Papa's idea to put her nickname on his car wasn't such a good one.

"Yes, officer, why?" Papa said.

"A woman claims that you were involved in a hit-and-run, that you hit her car and left the scene," the policeman said.

"Oh, no, it was a man driving and I gave him my insurance information," Papa said adamantly.

"Were you at the Sea First Bank on Beacon Hill this morning?" the policeman said. He could barely fit in our doorway; his head hovered like a giraffe over Papa.

"Yes, but the accident was not there. It was by Beacon Market," Papa said, his thick bifocals fogging up from the cold air.

"You will have to appear in traffic court," the cop said, handing Papa a ticket.

As the officer turned to leave, Papa started stuttering, scratching his gray hair, saying, "But, but, but why did that Black man turn me in?"

"Sir, it was a Caucasian woman who filed the complaint, you are mistaken," the officer said and left.

My mother closed the door, held her chest, saying, "*Diosko*—my God—we could've been killed today!"

"What happened?" *Kuya* and I asked. My brother grabbed the ticket and read it.

Mama replied, "*Ay, naku*, he had THREE car accidents today, not just one, but three!" she said louder, looking into Papa's eyes.

"Three? Where?" I asked.

"First one, he hit a telephone pole. I thought I was gonna die. Second, we were at the bank and he hit a parked car. Then later, we were leaving the market and he didn't see this other car when he pulled out of the driveway. Oh, I thought I was gonna die!"

"Was he driving fast?" *Kuya* asked.

"No, I was not! And I did not hit a car at the bank. It was a pole," Papa yelled.

"Well, obviously you did, and the lady must've seen you and written down your license plate, 'KaEmang!'" *Kuya* said with a flick of his wrist.

"Are you hurt? Do you want to see a doctor?" I said.

"No!" they screamed, a united front. They went into their bedroom to rest.

The next day, Papa asked me for his Tres Flores Pomade as he got dressed for the Filipino Community Center's Banquet and Ball. As a past president, he always wanted to look his best. I placed a dollop onto his left hand.

Then out of nowhere, he screamed, "I asked you to give me some pomade!"

"Um, Papa, it is right in your hand, can you not see it?" I said, flabbergasted.

"What?" He poked his finger on his palm to test if the grease was really there. "Oh, oh, well, I, I need some more then!" he stuttered.

I shook my head, not really thinking anything of it. On Sunday, Mama and Papa went to church. Sister Maria greeted Papa with a hug, and said, "*Manong*, you look a little tired. You left eye is kind of droopy, are you okay?"

Mama looked closer at Papa. They had been married for 30 years, but she had never seen him looking so tired. She whispered in Sister Maria's ear, but the beloved nun blurted out, "What? You had three car accidents the other day? You need to go see a doctor. Don't worry about being Eucharistic Minister today, we will find a replacement."

"Thank God for Sister Maria," Mama said when she returned home from the hospital. "The doctor said, 'Mr. Lawsin, it looks like you had a stroke. We are going to admit you and do more tests.' That is why he had all those accidents. *Diosko*, we could have died!"

The physical therapist and I had to teach Papa how to walk, see, speak, and write again. Printing and writing his name was the most difficult and took the longest for him to relearn, especially considering that he used to boast about winning awards for penmanship when he was a child. After four weeks, he eventually regained most of his abilities. When he appeared in traffic court, a judge revoked his driver's license. *Kuya* had to negotiate with our distant cousin, a car dealer, to end the lease on Papa's car. Even after seeing Papa's frail state and the court order, cousin car dealer gave them a hard time. However, Papa prevailed, and then began his 14-year escapade as a regular fixture on Seattle's Metro Bus System.

A year later, Papa behaved erratically—spending thousands of dollars each week on lotto tickets (first Washington State, then Australian Lottery). Telemarketing ads, placebo pills, and get-rich-quick television scams littered their mailbox and dining room. My siblings and I thought it was merely Papa's gambling addiction compounded by his search for the elusive "American Dream." Then he opened up and maxed out numerous credit cards in our youngest, developmentally disabled brother's name. That was when *Kuya* and I, along with our mother, had to legally intervene, and became our brother's guardians.

Papa became more irrational, but everyone dismissed it by calling him "*Matanda*:" Old. Some found it comically endearing, like at my California wedding. With suspenders showing through his sheer *piña barong*, Papa wore two left shoes that he had packed: one navy leather, one black patent. Before the ceremony, my nephew asked my sister, "Mom, why does Papa have two left feet?" When she pointed it out to our mother, Mama laughed so hard that she nearly peed in her Imelda-style gown. I wondered why Papa was frowning so hard during the photo shoot; his feet must have been aching! My brother-in-law let Papa wear his shoes while he slipped into sandals from the trunk of the car. During the first dance at the reception, Papa had forgotten how to waltz, which I did think was odd, since he was a champion waltz, tango, folk, and cha-cha dancer. Even before I knew how to walk, I had learned to dance standing on top of his feet.

The nonsensical, illegible, handwritten ten-page letters he sent me, some of them with postage due, should have been other clues. He forced my brother to type and email me those same letters. When Papa developed insomnia, he left long, repetitive messages on my voice mail at three o'clock in the morning, sometimes just screaming, "Hello? Hello! Hello!" over and over again for half an hour. He dropped his wallet over and over again, even when it was chained to his belt, until finally losing it. Several times. He lost his keys. Several times. He shuffled his feet so bad when he walked, that he was mugged twice getting off the bus. A thug ripped a gold chain right from Papa's neck, his St. Anthony pendant falling just inches from the sidewalk's sewer grate. Pretty soon, Papa couldn't balance his checkbook or even sign his name.

My mother worked as a cook. The year after she died, my father lost much of his appetite. He flew back to the Philippines by himself (against our wishes), nearly died from a fever, and came back two weeks early in a wheelchair, smelling like crap. Literally.

Half deaf, he yelled at all of his caregivers and refused to go to a nursing home, until he fell out of bed and took three hours to crawl to the telephone. Everyone told us, "He's 85. That's what happens when you get old." Or it was a result of his arthritis or gout. But then it happened again. In the hospital, *Kuya* thought he had heard Papa speaking in tongues, when he had actually reverted to speaking Waray-Waray, his provincial Visayan language that he never uttered in our home. Luckily, there were two Filipina nurses who could understand it.

A few months later, Papa caught pneumonia twice and could not walk. Then he couldn't eat. He forgot how to talk and how to swallow. The doctors gave us a choice: did we want to put a tube in his stomach to feed him, or did we want to enter him in end-of-life hospice care?

A week later, I flew home during Spring Break to see Papa. The day before I was supposed to fly back to work, he was short of breath and rushed by ambulance to a different hospital. That is when a young Pinoy doctor finally explained to us that Papa, lying down all day curled up in a ball, was in the last stage of Terminal Dementia, where the body forgets how to function. My cousins held vigil and brought food every day. Papa's friends and many of the hospital staff he had charmed came to visit and pray the Rosary. Our parish priest administered the last rites.

Five days later, right after our birthdays and our parents' wedding anniversary, *Kuya* wrote to our cousins, "Papa went to dance with Mama in heaven today."

With no worries about shoes.

AUNTIES WIN TRAM RIDE AT HANAUMA BAY

Jeanette Gandionco Lazam

Me and Bet was in Hawai'i for our monthly vacation. We figga we like stay at won fancy hotel dis year, so we pick 'em out and we decide on won Outrigger. Maybe not dat fancy eh, but at least different.

So den, afta check-in, we like go to Hanauma Bay to see all da odder malahini's, and watch dem as day watching us, trying to figga out how come dis local folks coming here? Always like to poke fun, eh!

So, we take won car ride up da mountain and we reach da Bay. Auweeeee! Crystal clear day, no clouds, and no pilikia wid no one and anyting. We stay about 2 hours den we getting bored, so we like take won tram up to where da car is parked. Befo' we go, we like break won mout on our musubi we bring wid us. Always gotta have sumptin to kau kau, nevah can tell wen you gonna get stuck up some where and you no have food! Next ting, you gonna start eating the grass, the wood off da snack bar, people inside da snack bar...you get it!

We just 'bout to get on won tram we won notice da tram all full and da last two seats left, won haoles already took 'em, so no mo' room fo' us. We big titas! Den won brah, he say, "Eh you. You like give up your seats fo' da aunties?" Da haoles look at one anodder all kine puzzled and dey not moving! (Wot! Cannot understand English!) So brah sez one mo' time, "Eh, you like give up won seat fo' da aunties, day kine heavy yah and need to take won tram up da mountain, odder wise if dey walk, day gonna die of won big, gigantic heart attack! So, gonna ask you one mo' time brah, give 'em up odder wise da

aunties death gonna be on your hands. Den you gonna have plenty pilikia!"
Oh, nevah see won haole move so fast!

GLOSSARY FOR NON-PIDGIN SPEAKERS

Afta	After
Anodder	Another
Anyting	Anything
Bet	Beth
Brah	Brother
Broke won mout	Ate food
Da	The
Den	Then
Dey	They
Figga	Figure
Haole	White person
Kau kau	Food
Kine	Kind, kind of
Malahini	Visitor, non-local
Mout	Mouth
Musubi	Sushi rice and Spam wrapped in Nori seaweed
Nevah	Never
Odder	Other
Pilikia	Problem
Sumptin	Something
Won	One

UNCLE PAUL LIVES ON MINNA STREET IN CENTRAL CITY

Juanita Tamayo Lott

Short, thick, black fingers clench a rolled copy of *Watchtower*!
As her mouth spews for the destruction of Sodom and Gomorrah on
Mid-morning wino whose thoughts concern only his trembling, gnarled hands
Balancing a jug of Ripple

Sensationalism of uncensored, uncut red passion blurs
Behind uncut pink carnations standing in their stalls
Left turn at the glass walls of Foster's 89 cents Chopped Beef Luncheon and
                                            Greyhound's toxic fumes
Bring me to Uncle Paul's

        CENTRAL CITY IS OUTSIDE THE CENTER
            MINNA STREET IS AN ALLEY UNCLE
        PAUL IS LEOPOLDO

Pungent odor of *bagoong* from the next-door flat cannot erase the urine of
                                            the front steps
I run up the 14 steps quickly and ring the bell
Exhaling only when the door is shut behind me
Down the dimly-lit hallway to the peeling yellow-painted kitchen
Uncle Paul cooks good pork adobo—chicken cacciatore-shrimp chow mein—
                                        barbecued steak and crab salad
He says he loves to cook anything for anybody, especially young people
And while his relatives, friends, and strangers feast, he downs his I.W. Harper

Juanita Tamayo Lott

He talks much of his white wife who took their baby daughter and their bank book
                                                                    and left him
                (his daughter must have her own daughters now) He
He talks more of goddamn-shit those car dealers and appliance salesman and
                how he's gonna die in two years without having paid for color t.v.
He talks loud and curses the Giants and Warriors and then puts down
                              his ice-filled glass
                                      with an emphatic thud

He rises to gather the leftover adobo and crab in a paper plate, wraps the plate in
wax paper and yesterday's Examiner want ads and ties this package with white string.

He goes down the steps, takes the lid off the garbage can
Carefully he sets the package and replaces the lid

Tonite, pass the broken glass and strewn candy wrapper and baseball cards of
The neighborhood Samoan and Filipino children,
An old man will stumble across my Uncle Paul's garbage can on
                                     Minna Street in Central City

First published in *Flips, A Filipino American Anthology*. 1971, Serafin Syquia, Editor

ATTITUDE ADJUSTMENT

Evelyn Luluquisen

Miles was more than happy to help me in my quest. We talked almost everyday, making sure to schedule our appointments. The checklist was long and it would take several months before we might begin to get some results. He wanted to as much as I did. We were ready.

"Thank you for returning my call. The doctor wants to see you before you start taking the prescription. Can you come in tomorrow?" asked the nurse.

"Yes, of course," I responded and noted the time and place for my appointment. I arrived early, anxious to know what the doctor was going to tell me.

"I reviewed the results of the sonogram. The images show that you have a septum in your uterus. It could be repaired with laser surgery, but there is no guarantee that you would be able to have a full-term pregnancy," said the doctor.

"Have I always had this septum in my uterus?" I responded.

"Yes. Twenty years ago the surgery would have been invasive and a full-term pregnancy may not have been possible. Here's a chart that shows the various types of septum. Yours looks like this one," said the doctor as she circled the picture of my septum.

"All these years I've wanted to have children and you tell me it's always been nearly impossible?"

"If you want, you could have surgery and take your chances. Or you might consider adoption."

"Wow, this is ironic. When I finally find a suitable partner who wants to have a child with me, I find out that my uterus is "out-of-order." First, I have to tell my friend. Adoption? We'll have to talk about it."

This is what I remember of that conversation in the doctor's office. I couldn't cry. Instead I felt a sense of relief. I have a medical condition. Somehow that lessened the stigma for me. I could explain that there is a septum in my uterus. When I put my two hands together to form a heart-shape, I could show that the crease at the top of the heart is the septum and the reason I am not able to have children.

Most family members look at me incredulously when I do my heart-shape demonstration and just nod their head as if I'm making an excuse. But I know what they are really thinking.

"Hi Auntie. Thank you for calling," I greeted Auntie Luming on the telephone with a smile on my face.

"Ess-mee-nee-yah?"

"No Auntie, this is Evelyn. Remember me?"

"Oh Eh-beh-leen! *Kumusta balasang ko*? (How are you my young lassie?) Is your mother home?

"Yes, Mom is home but she's asleep."

"Oh, okay. *Oy! Apay nag divorce ka?*" (Why did you get a divorce?)

"*Apay awan anak mo? Nabangles ti okim?*" (Why don't you have any children? Is your pussy stale?)

Auntie Luming had basically told me that a childless woman does not know how to please a man and does not know how to be submissive. I had to inhale deeply and hold my tongue so as not to say anything disrespectful to my elderly auntie. As I exhaled, I rationalized that she was projecting the kind of ridicule she experienced as an abused wife. Her husband was known as a "*palikero*" (playboy) who probably made her feel undesirable, a failure, and discarded. Perhaps she was repeating the same words her husband told her.

The truth is that my Auntie Luming was articulating what many in my family would not say or ask. Over the years I have endured side glances, comments and judgmental attitudes but, no matter how rude people were, I have always remained polite. The Ilocano language and culture is especially harsh for the way in which these judgmental attitudes are expressed. The Ilocano term for woman without child is "*balasang nga baket*" or loosely translated "old maid." In other words, a woman who does not bear a child will never mature into adulthood and is relegated to child status for her entire life. By the same token, a woman without a child is inadequate and incomplete.

I witnessed this attitude in my own family. My Dad's family followed tradition so that his youngest sister was not allowed to marry. As the youngest daughter in the family, her role was to care for her parents until they passed away. Even though she raised several nieces, nephews, grandnieces and grandnephews, she was called "*Nana Ubing*" (loosely translated in Ilocano "Child Mother"). When I met her in 1981 she was in her mid-70s, finally free of her care-giving responsibilities and ready to start a new life. Unfortunately, because of her status as a childless woman, she was not allowed to live independently in the Philippines and was shuffled around to different households in the United States. Now that I have the same "childless" status as Nana Ubing, I do not want the same thing to happen to me.

It's been over ten years since I got the news that I have a septum in my uterus. Finally the feelings of inadequacy as a "childless" woman no longer preoccupies my sense of womanhood. I enjoy my status as "Auntie" and "Tita." I enjoy my independence and take pride in all that I have accomplished thus far in life. In my observation, Filipino and American culture do not fully appreciate independent, single, childless elder women and men. Now I understand what the single *manongs* experienced. They were looked down upon by the Filipino community as they grew older. They were not given the respect or dignity to live independently in safe, decent, affordable housing. Our *manongs* were not always welcome and given a space in our own Filipino family homes. Think about it. Homes with separate living quarters are called "in-law apartments." I do not know of anywhere in Filipino and American culture that refers to a special place allocated for aunties and uncles who are single, childless elders.

I believe that attitudes towards single, childless elder women and men in Filipino and American culture and society need to change. Being without children does not mean that a person is inadequate or incomplete. Society needs to understand that it is by either by choice or circumstance that factor into a person's life when it comes to marital status or children. In other words, no one is at fault and there should be no judgment.

As I approach retirement age and senior citizen status, I grow more concerned about how single, childless women, in particular Filipino women, are treated in the United States and in the Philippines. In my ideal world, single, childless elders would continue to live in compounds close to their family and friends. I envision inter-generational communities with mutual support. As a live-in caregiver for my elderly mother, I know the value of living in an inter-generational community. Right now I have immediate family living on the same city block and more family members who live in the region. My brother, sisters, cousins, nieces and nephews can be called upon to provide support. My nieces and nephews love their *lola* dearly and brighten up her life. Our households can easily get together to share our home-cooked meals and exchange home-grown vegetables from our gardens.

Single, childless women and men deserve to be treated with respect and not be treated as oddities in Filipino and American society. Mutually supportive communities and families should be the norm, not the exception.

GIFT OF PLUMS

Rebecca Mabanglo-Mayor

When summer days begin to wane toward Fall, it's hard to stay indoors. It must have been that way for my dad those Sunday afternoons in the early '70s, when he would turn our big blue Coronet 500 sedan out of the church parking lot in the opposite direction of home. He spent his workdays verifying invoices and his nights balancing the family checkbook or watching the football game on TV. Saturdays were his garden days, pulling up weeds and mending bean trellises. Even on Sundays, chores needed to be done, but only if he drove straight home after Mass. Maybe the sunlight would strike his face as he left the church and he'd breathe deep the offshore wind, then it would be settled in his mind. No chores today.

He and Mom settled themselves on shiny leather bucket seats, and me in the back, the seat all to myself. I was probably nine or so and if I stretched out and lay down on the seat, my head and feet would never touch the door, the seat was so wide. Old Thumper, as we called my dad's car, didn't have air conditioning, so we'd roll down the windows and let the air billow in. Warm air that didn't so much cool, but moved the air around and made us feel a little bit better than the closeness of a car shut from the world.

When we hit the corner of Old 99 and 320th, Dad would tap his wedding band on his left hand in counterpoint to the rhythm he tapped with his class ring on his right hand, and we'd wait for the light to change from red to green. I'd try to guess our destination from where he steered the car next —east meant Auburn and the search for fresh fruits and vegetables at old truck farms that dotted the valley. South meant visiting cousins in Tacoma while north usually meant visiting my mother's parents in Seattle. Any direction, though, meant a long ride by my nine-year-old reckoning, and I'd doze, listening to my parent's conversation weave in and out of songs on the radio. My parents speak Tagalog, a Filipino dialect with rolling tones that rose and fell around and through the strains of "Strangers in Paradise" and "How Much is that Doggie in the Window." As I drifted to sleep, their voices mixed with the drone of tires on pavement, turned hollow and distant, then melted into dreams of yellows and pinks and greens. Often I'd wake in time to hear my dad shut off the engine and saw the world in shades of blue, the brightness of waking up too much for me at first. Blinking, I'd sit up to see where we'd arrived.

Sometimes I'd find us in front of a low-slung craftsman with a simple porch and picture window facing the street. Stepping out of the car, I'd get quieter inside myself, cautious in unfamiliar surroundings. My parents, on the other hand, would be excited and smiling, knocking carefully at the door, then opening it if it was unlocked. I'd follow them into a small foyer, then through the dining room of the darkened house. Like a closed-up car, the room felt hot and cramped, the dark wood furniture and the scent of mothballs giving the space an unlived-in feel. The voices rose and fell again as my parents exchanged greetings with the owners of the house. I heard "Auntie Dora!" and "How big you are!" and "Are you hungry?" and my caution turned into a feeling of boredom as I realized there were no other children in this house, and it would be adults talking over and around me in a language I didn't speak.

But as dark as the house was inside, the terraced back yard was always bright and sunny. A small kitchen garden was grown on the first level nearest the kitchen—peas and corn, tomatoes and squash, spinach and bok choy. Then down the next terrace were the trees, three plum trees and one apple tree, each bursting with fruit. Actually they weren't plum trees but Italian prune trees, which always confused me a bit because to my mind, prunes were those oversized, wrinkly raisins my mother complained about having to eat every so often because she felt "a bit stopped up." And come to think of it, Italian prunes, in the garden of a Filipino, they could probably be called anything we wanted. So they were The Plums, oval and dusty purple, soft and sweet. Small, too. I could eat one in two bites, carefully avoiding the seed for my mother's sake.

Uncle Sammy, Auntie Dora's husband, handed Dad a white bucket and he trudged down the hill to fill it. Their conversation wouldn't lose a beat as Uncle Sammy trailed behind, stopping occasionally to pull up a bunch of plantain growing in the path. The soft green leaves would come home with us too, for throwing in a pot of water with chicken and spice. But my tongue was set on the flavor of sun-warmed plums. Candy and treats from packages could be had any old time at the store, but these plums only came around once a year, and once the trees were done, you'd have to wait. When the white bucket returned to the kitchen and boredom was forgotten, I sat on a kitchen chair, feet dangling below as I ate plum after plum after purple, sweet plum.

Years later, after I finished high school and had gone off to college, I nearly forgot about those plums. Time squeezed and compressed into the busyness of creating a life away from my family, away from leisurely drives to truck farms and backyard gardens. I forgot about how blue the world looked when I woke from a nap in the car. I forgot about the sunlight slanting through dusty windows to strike against the dark, curved furniture carved in an older age. I forgot about those summer drives and the taste of sun-warmed sweetness on my tongue. I forgot, that is, until my dad called me one late summer afternoon and asked if we wanted some plums. He had a bumper crop and needed help to eat them all before they went to compost.

A few days later, my husband and I pulled up to my parents' house, and once again I was sitting on a barstool in the kitchen, feet dangling as I munched purple treasures, all sun-warmed and sweet.

Rinsing another batch of plums in the sink, my mom told me that Uncle Sammy and Auntie Dora were the ones who introduced my parents to each other and later were sponsors at their wedding.

"When we built this house, Uncle Sammy and Uncle Fred planted the trees in the backyard," she said. "They brought us seedlings from their trees for good luck."

She went on to explain that neither of the men were actually uncles of either of my parents. Sammy was Mom's distant cousin and Fred was from her dad's hometown. They were both old timers, schoolboys who'd come to the states when the Philippines was still a protectorate of the U.S. in the early 1920s. They'd made it good in America, first getting married and then buying their own homes where they could plant trees, a sure sign of permanence and prosperity.

Neither lived to see the crop Dad offered us that year, but as I sat listening to their stories, I realized that growing things was about hope for the future, of planting a small thing into good soil so the plant will grow up strong. Gardening was about continuity too, from seed to fruit to harvest and back to seed again, especially for a Filipino garden because seeds and saplings were part of the community, a way to keep together. A way to stop the forgetting that comes from separation.

When my husband and I bought our own house a few years later, a low-slung craftsman with enough bedrooms for our two children and us, Dad brought over baby trees from his orchard, the second generation of Uncle Sammy's trees. After the trees were planted, Dad explained how to cover the seedlings that first winter to help them survive.

"Take good care of them," he said. "And you'll have plums just like us."

As we stood near the seedlings, we watched the children chase each other up and down the lawn. I wondered how much of the day they would remember and if they would match their childhoods to the growth of our trees. Soon, we all hoped, they would pluck the warm fruit from the trees in their hands, pop them in their mouths to relish the sun and sweetness on their tongues.

AGTAWID (INHERITANCE)

Lisa Suguitan Melnick

In the summer of 1976, I moved into my grandparents' house in the Richmond District. I had been awarded a scholarship to study in Japan, but the program would not begin for two more months. For me, a university student, the meager funds remaining in my bank account might be just enough to cover first month's rent and a cleaning deposit for an apartment that did not yet exist. Thus, right now, having a room in my grandparents' home was a blessing.

To and from work I went, using a student Fast Pass on the 5 McAllister and 28-19th Avenue bus lines. In the evenings, together with Grandpa, Grandma, and the Uncles, we ate Filipino meals of *pinakbet* and steak; milkfish and cauliflower; *higado* with fresh greens; salmon heads and spinach, with lots of steaming hot rice. They gifted me with comfort in my belly and fed culture to my spirit. From our mealtimes together, I inherited a sense of belonging.

On Sunday mornings, Grandma and I walked to 9 A.M. mass at St. Thomas the Apostle Church, five blocks from her bright orange Victorian with chocolate brown trim on 35th Avenue.

"Is my house pretty?" she asked me each time we got to the bottom of the stairs. Together we would turn around, arm-in-arm, and look up at the house. "What do you think of the color, Lisa-Tita?"

"Maybe go with a little lighter color next time, Grandma."

She would just squeeze my arm and say, "My house is pretty, don't you think?"

"Yes, Grandma," I'd smile.

"Really?"

"Yes, really, Grandma," placing my hand over hers.

From her, I learned about hard-earned privilege to own a home. She and Grandpa had paid cash for it during the Depression. I learned about the discipline of saving up money from their restaurant, simply named, "1550 Geary." I realized their perseverance, working and saving money during an era when —eventually— it became legal for Filipinos to own a piece of property in their own name. After years of having the same conversation with Grandma, about whether her house was pretty, while standing arm-in-arm looking up at it, eventually I got it: that her house, bright orange with chocolate brown trim, was indeed beautiful beyond dispute.

"O-kay, let's go to church now," she'd smile, satisfied.

Grandma liked to sit near the back, on the left side, beside the heaters. The hissing from the pipes reminded me how hot it was in those pews. By the middle of the sermon, I'd be fanning myself with whatever misalette booklet I could find, to keep from fainting. I felt even hotter when I glanced over at my grandma, who always wore a wool coat, a scarf around her neck, and a silk bandana around her head—because we were in God's house. When the baskets made their way down the aisle, Grandma would meticulously fold four dollar bills—one from each of the uncles, one from her and then one from Grandpa. She'd slide them into a colored collection envelope, neatly lick it shut, and then hand it to me.

"Drop it there in the basket when it comes down the row," she'd whisper, pointing toward it with her lips.

After church, Grandma and I took the 38 Geary ten blocks to Cala Foods to buy groceries. When we returned home, she would write her long division calculation directly on the receipt, dividing the cost of the groceries four ways. My grandparents and two unmarried great-uncles lived as housemates.

When it came to expenses, each contributed equally to the household. Sliding the receipt showing her long division calculations across the Formica dining table, she'd say to the uncles, "Here's the bill for the groceries. Fifteen dollars and seventy-four cents divided by 4. Your share is three dollars and ninety-three cents." Uncle Anong would take the red Folger's coffee can from on top of the refrigerator and bring it to the table. Grandma would drop in her and Grandpa's share: $7.86 exactly. "Wait a minute. Here's a penny," she'd say, her index finger sorting through coins in her palm.

Grandma carried a wallet but that wasn't where she kept all her money. Instead she pulled the paper bills from a recycled postal envelope placed in a secret pocket inside her purse. Each of the uncles would add their money to the can, making change as needed. The balancing of the household expenses and responsibilities was a ritual. Witnessing their daily ritual with money, I inherited mindfulness about the value of the hard-earned rewards of work.

The time came for me to depart for Japan. With my last paycheck, I converted $500 into Traveler's checks and took $100 in cash for transportation to the airport. I packed the money deep into my backpack along with my passport and round trip plane ticket from my scholarship sponsor.

The next morning, as I was bringing my suitcase down from my room, Grandpa, Grandma, Uncle Anong, and Uncle Pepe walked me to the door. Grandpa put one hand on my arm and handed me a white letter-sized envelope with the other.

"Here, Lisa. Something from all of us—Grandma, me, Uncle Pepe, and Uncle Anong. During your studies in Japan, 'Make It Nice.' We are proud of you!" He pushed the side of my head affectionately, nodding his approval.

"Make It Nice." He always said that to us grandkids whenever he wanted to encourage us to be our very best. Looking at their faces at the door, I suddenly felt apprehensive about leaving them for two months, and blurted out something silly like, "Wait for me to come back and we'll go grocery shopping together, okay?"

Grandpa's answer provided reassurance. "Yes, it's okay. Go ahead now!"

I slid the envelope into my jacket pocket, kissed them again, turned and left before he saw tears.

I closed my eyes as the airport bus headed out on Fulton Street and through the Golden Gate Park to get to 19th Avenue. When we got onto the freeway, I opened the envelope. Inside was a stack of money. I fingered through the bills, adding them up. At first I was puzzled by the combination of ones and fives, and the random amount.

$37.00.

All at once, I pictured the red Folger's coffee can on top of the refrigerator. I imagined the four of them—Grandma, Grandpa, Uncle Pepe, and Uncle Anong—emptying out all the money and coins from the coffee can onto the table. Money they had collected from putting in their share of the groceries; calculating what was still needed for household expenses; skimming some from what remained of the money, for me; adding in their pocket change; converting the coins nicely into paper money; and finally, placing the resulting amount into a white letter-sized envelope.

I was astounded by how deeply their gift symbolized the fruits of their hard work, their high regard for education—my education—something that had not been so easy to complete for them.

A simple white envelope, with dollars from my grandparents and great-uncles, each sheet of money stacked up creating the floor on which I could plant my own feet so firmly. $37.00. Everlasting *Agtawid*.

OUT THE BACK DOOR

Lisa Suguitan Melnick

I remember the final night of my mother's funeral wake. As the last drawn-out "A-a-men" croaked from the priest's mouth, Auntie Lucrecia decisively grabbed my hand and led me out the back door, away from the East Chapel of McAvoy and O'Hara Mortuary. The fresh air pierced my uncovered head. Had I stopped breathing within the stale heaviness of the chapel? My eyes remained squeezed shut; pressing my nose into Auntie's arm, I followed blindly. Feel the windy Geary Street traffic. It rustles up under my slip blowing my dress like a billowed sail. The heavy air from the parlor sticks to my face. Feels like a maroon-colored velvet curtain pulling tightly around my nose and mouth, wrapping round and round—the flat-nosed little girl in the dark green dress with a scalloped white collar. Curtain swaddles my skinny brown body down around my chapped, scabby knees. Balls of dust tumble from between the pleats, dropping down into my lace bobby socks. The dust balls are "pom-pom" bugs with a life of their own; now, the curtain tucks its excess length underneath my new Mary Jane shoes. Feeling smothery around my nose, I walk as if shackled at the ankles, shuffling on tippy toes behind Auntie Lucrecia in fainting steps. Unable to move my arms, unable to feel my body under the thick velvet curtain, I hope that I'm not really here at all.

Just moments before being led out the back door, ticking coming from an uncle's wristwatch—the kind with little dashes for the numbers—made me aware of each achy second that passed. He shuffled by the front pew where I sat with my little brother. Uncle dabbed his oily forehead with his hankie and made his way toward my mother's casket, his walker landing three times on the fleur-de-lys carpeting, Tap. Sh-h-oop. Tap. Sh-h-oop. Tap. Sh-h-oop. Finally, he arrived at the edge of the casket, close enough to lean forward and gaze into my mother Anita's face.

"Oh, my goodness, 'Nita. Only thirty-three years old, darling. Why did you hab to die so young?" he sobs in his Ilocano accent. His wailing causes Grandma to come forward to join in. "What will the children do without their mother, honey dear? Look at them. So young! *Ay nako*."

Grandma resumes wailing where she had begun four days earlier. Right in the middle of the Girls section of Sears Roebuck, while shopping for funeral clothes for me, she had told every salesgirl who passed, "My granddaughter needs a dress. She is my granddaughter. For a funeral. Do you have black in her size? Da mother died." Grandma cried, yet managed to continue rambling through her sobs. "Mmm-hmm. We need a black dress. A black sweater. For the funeral of her mother."

She grabbed my forearm, pumping it within her hand as if checking the ripeness of a mango. She accepted each sympathetic response from the salesgirls as an invitation to add more details. "She was very sick. In the hospital for over one week this time. She died. Last Thursday."

Tactfully the salesgirls kept their eyes on my grandmother and off of me. My stomach, holding a jagged pit the size of my fist, sent nauseating heat to my profoundly heavy chest. Grandma settled on a pine green dress with a white collar, black lace bobby socks, a grey coat, and a new pair of size 10 patent leather Mary Jane shoes. From that day on, I would forever detest shopping.

Now sitting in the family section of the funeral parlor, separated from the people, I replayed that shopping scene while I looked down at my lap, noticing that the pine green dress had subtle triangular patterns in the fabric. I avoided looking at anyone in the funeral parlor by moving my eyes to a spot just above my mother's casket. I focused hard on the lower left corner of the brushed silver crucifix of Jesus hanging against the rosewood backdrop. Two nights earlier, when I had first seen the grayish pallor of the face of this woman in the beautiful rose-colored casket, heavily made-up and fake-looking, I pitched backward, my mind racing too fast for my body. I thought I was in the wrong parlor because that woman lying in the casket could not be my mother. Wait. Did my mother die or is this a sad dream?

I remember that her facial expression was odd: lips pinched together a bit tight and turned slightly downward, edges of her eyes turning down the same way, like they were about to cry. Was she in pain at the end? No, her expression means she knew her life was to end, I decide.

"Oh, no, I am not going to be able to see my precious kids." To remind us to obey our Dad.

"Please bring the kids to see me one last time." To tell us that Mommy is feeling alright now, but that she has to leave.

"Be tough girl. Strong Girl. Smart Girl." To tell me to take good care of my little brother. To encourage me to do well in school.

"You're a good big sister." To kiss my cheeks, and whisper in my ear, "Don't worry. Mommy will always be near."

Suspended there, I am the only person in the room, my eyeballs distracted by a movement overhead, where I find... myself... fluttering on wings above my own body, hovering above the impending last night of my mommy's Rosary—the Rosary of this woman in the pink casket. I close my eyes. If I sing to myself, will I open my eyes and be someplace else, anyplace else but here?

Three six nine, the goose drank wine
The monkey chewed tobacco on the street car line
The line broke, the monkey got choked
And they all went to Heaven on a little green boat.*

*Shirley Ellis, "The Clapping Song" 1965

"C'mon, let's go out." Dad's sister, my Auntie Lucrecia, takes my hand assuringly, as she turns me toward her and wipes away my tears, guides me out the back door of the east parlor onto Geary Street, and buttons up that ugly, grey poodle coat against the damp December air.

BEAUTY QUEENS

Veronica Montes

I once saw a movie where beautiful, long-haired girls knelt on a golden beach grieving the loss of loved ones. They ripped out their hair and wailed while blood ran down the sides of their faces and onto the flowers they wore around their necks. My auntie Cely is wailing like that now, wailing like her life has been coming to an end for weeks and this is her last chance to make an impression on the world. My mother glares at her and mutters an incredible string of cuss words under her peppermint breath. I keep a light hold on her wrist in case she tries to jump up and gore her sister through the stomach with the horns I imagine she keeps hidden under her thick black hair. This image makes me laugh, which I shouldn't do, considering this is her mother's—my *lola*'s—wake and everyone is kind of sad, really.

Lola died in her sleep after emitting a loud and prolonged sigh. Someone let it slip that she was naked, a fact that thrills my cousin Girlie and me to no end. Out of thirty-eight cousins, Girlie is my favorite, my true and kindred spirit. We were born two days apart in the same hospital and often pretend we were switched in the nursery, which would actually make me, her, and her, me. I think about that a lot.

My mother calms herself by taking deep, exaggerated breaths. She and Auntie Cely do not get along. Not with each other or any of their sisters or, less surprisingly, with any of their brothers' wives.

"You're okay?" I ask.

"I'd be fine," she says, massaging her own neck, "if your aunt would shut up." She puts a hand to her hair, and then dips it quickly into her purse to pull out a mirror so she can check her lipstick. Without looking at me she says, "Zeny, go sit with your *lolo*."

This task requires walking by Auntie Cely's husband Mark, an ex-Marine who rambles off the names of islands and provinces I can't even spell and who bores Girlie and me to death with accounts of what he calls his "previous life in Southeast Asia." His conversations always begin, "Once in Cotabato..." or "My good friends in Bohol..." He used to kiss Lola's hand, sometimes raising it to his forehead and holding it there for a moment while he closed his eyes. Lola would flare her nostrils and head for the kitchen.

When I was little, I'd beg Mark to come see my turtle, my sterling silver locket, my Holly Hobbit lunchbox. Afterwards, he'd hand me five dollars. "For candy," he always said. At my seventh birthday party, he walked into our family room with a box so big it made everyone gasp. Inside were three party dresses, a fake fur coat (in white), and a Barbie doll with a large suitcase. The suitcase opened to reveal the interior of an airplane where Barbie could serve passengers coffee and tea from a rolling cart.

Mark and Auntie Cely moved to Arizona soon after, and they didn't come home until I was fourteen. I regarded Mark as a stranger. "Shame on you," my mother said. "Look at him when he speaks to you." So I did. I looked at his nose, his forehead, his hair—anywhere but his eyes. Twice today he has wedged himself between Girlie and me, pretending like he needs to get to the other side of the room. "What would you call this sandwich?" he says with a smile, scooting sideways and managing to press up against both of us.

Lolo sits in the first pew and keeps perfectly still as people whisper in his ear and place envelopes of money in his breast pocket. Sometimes he turns and stares at Auntie Cely, willing her into silence. She looks tragically lovely, what with her hair a little mussed and her eyes brimming with tears. She has planned it that way; she is brilliant that way.

All afternoon, Lolo has kept each of his hands on top of each of his knees, bracing. "*Hija*, who sent that terrible arrangement?" he says, pointing with his lips. He is talking about a wilting wreath of red carnations.

"I think it was the Santos family." I whisper so nobody will hear.

Lolo nods. "You know," he says, "your grandmother was a beauty queen in the Philippines."

"I know," I say.

"There was a parade and all the little pink and white flowers caught in her hair. She took them out later and kept them in a dish on her dresser."

I've heard this a million times. I want something else. I want to hear about how Lola loved to kneel in the garden and sing to her flowers. I want to hear about the time she kicked the neighborhood pervert in the balls or how she quietly gave birth to Uncle Roly as she hid from Japanese soldiers in the attic of the old house. I wait, but he doesn't offer anything more.

"Is that all?" I finally say, pulling myself up and looking him in the face. "Is that it? My grandmother was a beauty queen?"

He stares at me like I am the biggest disappointment of his life. I return the favor.

Once when I was seven years old I woke up obsessed with the word "biscuit" (the week before it was "crisp"). I sat in front of the mirror saying it over and over again. I liked the sound of it as it came out of my mouth, my tongue wrapping around the hard edges, hitting against the back of my two front teeth when the final "t" sounded. I was so overwhelmed that I mixed together oatmeal, flour, and orange juice and made one hundred and five small biscuits. When no one would eat them I cried and brought them to my lola. She laid them out in her garden like a thousand gifts and held me on her lap while we watched the birds feast.

Girlie likes that story.

She's sitting on a couch in the foyer with her feet propped up on an ottoman. She can tell it's me by the click of my footsteps. "Is Auntie Cely still throwing a fit?" she says. She is staring at the ceiling, probably dying for a cigarette.

"Can't you hear her?"

She listens for a moment and closes her eyes, nodding. "What did Lolo say?"

"Oh, you know: 'It rained flowers,' and all that."

"If I have to hear about that one more time, I will vomit," she says. "Tell me a story."

The people who have been milling around all afternoon smiling at us like we're orphans, are drifting out. They leave in groups and pretty soon it's just the two of us sitting on the couch with the rest of the family inside, staring at Lola. Then Mark walks up.

"Hi girls," he says. He salutes with one hand, while clutching his paper cup in the other. I'd bet a thousand dollars he didn't get that cup of coffee himself. Auntie Cely brought it to him, or maybe one of our mothers. They always hover around him, making sure he's comfortable, happy.

Girlie and I raise our eyebrows and cross our arms over our chests, but Mark stays put. Mark is unfazed.

"So," he says, "I understand your lola was a beauty queen in the Philippines."

"No kidding," I say.

He smiles and turns towards Girlie. "I believe your mother can boast of a crown or two."

"Wow," Girlie says, rolling her eyes.

Girlie's the best.

"Beautiful girls in the Philippines," Mark adds. "In fact, I met a number of beauty queens when I was there. Zamboanga, Cebu, all over. And I certainly married into a family that's full of them." He smiles; he winks.

It's like I'm watching this from the other side of the room. I can see us straining our necks to look up at him and him, smiling down at us. I stand up and say it: "My *lola* was a beauty queen. The women you met were prostitutes," I say. "Why can't you tell the difference?"

"What are you saying, Zeny? What is this all about?"

"You're not fooling any of us except maybe Auntie Cely," I say. "We all know you're one of those ass-hole Marines that kept the Olongapo bargirls busy swiveling their hips." I raise my arms and swivel my hips.

Girlie stares at me with unabashed love and devotion. She stands up; she pinches my arm.

"You wait just a minute now," Mark says, not even blushing, not even embarrassed. "I treated every woman I met with the utmost respect."

"Oh, you mean 'conduct befitting' and all that? What does that even mean? You said 'thank you, Miss' when you finished your business?" He stares at me with his mouth wide open.

"Yeah," Girlie says.

Girlie's the best.

BABAYLAN IN PLAYLAND BY THE SEA

Oscar Peñaranda

The stupidest thing that the city of San Francisco ever did was to get rid of Playland by the Sea, with its Funhouse Fat Laughing Lady with freckles and red hair, its grand towering Ferris Wheel, and the formidable Salt and Pepper Shaker Loop—where he, as a teenager, once discovered too late not to have anything in one's pockets because they will all fall down: coins, pens, whatever, when the ride turns you upside down violently and fearfully. Hot dog stands steaming in the night and the carnival atmosphere everywhere and all around, the various sounds (barks) of laughter floating in the air. It was a mini Disneyland right across the misty Pacific Ocean, the Great Highway and the Cliff House, a turn of the twentieth century restaurant made of brass and dark wood. Unfortunately, Playland was swallowed up by the waves of greed. Speculation, they called it. So they closed it down, built apartments and condos instead to make more money. Joy subsided quickly like the foams from among and along those silver-crested waves. No more mermaids beckoned from the sea. Where once it shimmered in the summers of the City, the area now is a very quiet place and deserted. Lonesome winds frequent it. Condominiums and apartments were put on the site where Playland used to be. Those apartments and condominiums have never been fully occupied. In due time, desolation took over the place and no children were ever seen near it. That was the day the magic died in Playland by the sea. Songs and stories will be the only remnants of those days. This is one of them.

Priday Night Walker called his trusted friend Amador one day during prom season and told him to get ready for a double date that he, Priday, is arranging.

"You gotta go on a double date with me, pal." He said with his phony Texas (Filipino) accent. Priday Night Walker, a Filipino mestizo whose white U.S. citizen father was in the service, found himself growing up mostly right in the heart of Texas, of all places. His father was transferred to San Francisco only six years ago. He got to know everybody fast. He was a very social guy as you can tell by what folks called him.

"I don't got a "date," Amador reminded him.

"I know that," answered Priday quickly. "I don't know why; you got the looks.

Look at me...Pry-day Night Walker..."

"No thanks."

"I just don't know what it is they see in me, but..."

"It aint the looks, that's for sure."

"But I always got a girl, right? And seein' that I knew you wouldn't have one, and seein' that the prom is already this Sarday nat...I got you one."

He was right, the fucker. Compared to Priday's social life, Amador felt at times that he would languish in loneliness for the rest of his obscure life.

It seemed that his (Priday's) date's parents won't allow the two of them on a date alone. Amador did not know whether the parents had heard of Priday's reputation or not. They would however permit her to go on a double date with her girlfriend (and family trusted companion) who will turn out to be his, Amador's, blind date.

"We'll spend for everything," Priday told Amador. "I'll take care of expenses," he said.

"What about for the date?" Amador asked.

"Not the expenses that don't involve me, *pare*. You gotta cough that up yourself, brother. I'll just provide the merchandise; you gotta pay for the maintenance. Dont be *kuripot*, man. C'mom, you gotta fork out something. Show some class, man. You're buying her a corsage, right?"

Amador, the ever-accomodating (in his mind) young man of seventeen that he was, said, "Yes, of course." Amador himself had just graduated. His graduation celebrations and activities were nothing to brag about. In fact, it was nothing at all, period. Just a kiss from his mother and a controlled smile from his father. He had not gone to his school prom, though the priest, his Saint Ignatius High School English teacher, had offered him a couple of names from his list of Mercy High School girls. The same priest had procured him one before on the Sadie Thompson Dance. Her name was Anne Farmer and her straight, long, red hair still had him remembering. The truth is that Amador had hinted to his mom about going to the prom, but she picked up on it right away and said, "Nating doing! No money for all dis *kalokohans*. It's not enough that you go to the most expensive school in San Francisco. You have to pick the most expensive event *pa*!"

"Ma, this is the prom. And I didn't pick the school. You guys did."

"Not me," she said and cast a furtive glance toward his father who was reading the newspaper while watching the news on the television in the *sala*, as he, with his Giants baseball cap on, was listening to the baseball game on the radio in the kitchen.

"They're paying for the whole thing, Ma."

"Who are 'they,' *ha*?"

"I guess their family, Priday's girlfriends' family, or her girlfriend's girfriend's family. I don't know. All I know is that I, I mean we, I mean you, are not paying for a centavo, Ma. *Wala. Libre lahat.*"

"*Siyet*," she curtly said.

And he kissed her on both cheeks, making *gigil* noises and grabbed her shoulder and started massaging it and shaking it until she wrinkled her forehead and started screaming for him to stop. "*Hoy! Hoy!*" And laughing he slowly let her go.

"*Siyet*", she said again, regaining some control and fixing herself up.

The ride after the prom was rather quiet. He had danced with his date Maria a few times only. He should have danced more, he knew, but it was too late now. Priday pulled over by the diner with the big dachsund hot dog on top of it by 48th Avenue, near the Great Highway. Priday and his prom date quickly disappeared into the Laughing Lady's entrance gate, leaving the two alone. Amador and Maria sat down at a small eating place and as they were ordering the food, Amador started noticing Maria. He started listening well to what she was saying, as he slowly chewed on his fish and chips with a sprinkling of vinegar. The jukebox was playing "Sally Go 'Round the Roses" and she was humming and oo-oowing a bit. They finished their meals and smiling at each other (as the Rocky Fellers were busting out "Killer Joe"), walked outside into the lights-studded mist. They walked somewhat awkwardly through parts of Playland to cross the Great Highway onto Ocean Beach, passing the Laughing Lady, the dart and balloon games, the shooting galleries, and the cotton candy wagons, till they confronted the giant Ferris Wheel with all its lights and colors and slow, creaky turning. Everything must have been turning in Maria's inside, too, because she suddenly said:

"Someday, I'll have my name in lights. Keystone Korner, Black Hawk, Blue Note. You never know, right? Why not?"

"Sure, why not?" He said. "You're a good singer. I can tell by your humming you got soul. I can't sing, but I can tell soulful singing."

"To sing, I think, to really sing your own, you gotta do it with passion. But you gotta have a broken heart or two under your belt to have that passion. I think. I don't know what I'm saying." She looked up at him smiling a bit and took his arm to cross the street to the ocean's side.

She was looking up at him and beyond him, at the sky, with white-edged clouds bathed and drifting by the silvery moon, seawind blowing, foaming waves pounding, her chiffon dress puffed billowing with the billows of the sea.

After they've crossed, he said, "Maybe you can teach me to sing. Think it's possible? Can anyone learn? I'm pretty hopeless. I might scare away all the mermaids by singing off-tune."

"Nonsense. Anybody can sing. My niece is tone-deaf and I taught her."

"Wow, you're a teacher, too. You're gifted."

She looked at him straight and clear and kindly. They were stepping on sand now. "You're the gifted one." She was looking through him, beyond him, into the moonlit sea. "You'll write about us and someday people will read them and someday, maybe, one will come to know someone like me. You're the gifted one." She moved a little closer to him and walked in his rhythm, taking bigger steps. "The waves, the ocean, the sea, will wipe them all out immediately, but the spirit of our footprints will still be in these sands because you will write about them, I can tell. I know a little bit about you before from Priday and them. Research is good, right?"

"When before, or before when?"

"Before before *pa*."

"Wow! A budding private investigator, too. 77 Sunset Strip, Hawaii Five-O, female Ponce Pons!"

"More like *Paway* Five-O. I'm Ilokana. My mother's Tagalog, though. She named me after the legendary Maria of Mount Makiling because I was born in the calm right after a storm. I like to know what I'm getting into, of course, before I jump into anything.

"With a practical and desperate friend like Priday, one has to excavate a little oral history on his double date choices," she smiled, her red lips accentuating her scarlet and gold shawl. With a slight change of tone she said, "You keep writing. You keep us alive."

"That's funny," he answered. "Everyone tells me to dream another dream, to stop writing. I'll be broke all my life, they say. No one is interested in reading about Filipinos, especially Filipinos, they all tell me. Don't know if I should even consider it now. My own family..."

"Consider it? You talk as if you have a choice. You don't. And you're good. I read some of your poems that you write for your friends to the girl of their dreams, or the object of their lustful affection. Some are too good to send away. I hope you keep all of them."

"Yeah, some of them won't appreciate the poems, huh?"

"Oh, they'll appreciate them all right. Every one of them. A girl appreciates those things. But not necessarily for the same reasons."

"Really? Do they know it is not from their aspiring suitors?"

"Of course, they do. C'mon, they all know they came from you."

"I'll make sure to keep them all from now on."

They took off their shoes and started laughing. He tried to carry her pair but she would not let him. "It's all right. I'll carry them. They're my shoes, after all." The night was all a splash in spindrifts brought by the wind and waves. They strolled on the sands of the silver-ladened seascape. He noticed the moon, though not yet full, was bright and it made his gaze wander towards the horizon. It was during this gaze that a strange surge of romantic feeling overwhelmed him. It was prom night after all, and he suddenly swept Maria off her feet and scooped her up, carrying her as they both almost fell. Regaining his balance, he continued carrying her, trying to keep up a conversation. He noticed the silveriness of things as the moon momentarily got in his eye. It took his attention for a split second and then that was all because a wave, a giganitc one, rose like a monster from the sea and it was heading straight for them. Terror-stricken and instinctively obeying the most formidable human urge, that of self-preservation, he forgot everything and ran away from the great wave, toward the Great Highway. But of course, he forgot the bundle he had in his arms a few seconds ago, the object of his romanticism. He looked down at his empty arms and looked back and saw Maria squirming to get up from the water's edge like a cockroach on its back trying to get right side up. Coming to his senses, he rushed to her, shouting apologies before he even got to her and picked her up.

"Not just our footprints, now," Maria said laughing in her surprise, "but my body prints, too," brushing off the sands and water from herself. "I was shaking like a cockroach out there."

"Or a mermaid," he said.

When he had gathered her in his arms safely and things started to look right-side up again, he clumsily added,"You're a wise one. With a hell of a sense of humor, too."

"But you," she touched both his hands and turned them palm up, "with these soft hands, are the gifted one. Remember that."

"You're all wet?"

"Just a little."

"Wanna go back to the diner and change in the bathroom?"

"Change to what, my slip or shawl?" and then she thought for a while. "Why not?

I'll just put my coat over it. C'mon. No. Let's go in the Cliff House. I'll change there."

When she came out of the Cliff House, she came out all colorful and *babaylan*-like. She looked like she belonged in the richy, classy Cliff House (by her carriage and posture), yet she did not belong in the Cliff House (by her splash of many colors), too bold to neatly fit the ambiance. Biblical, yet pagan. Folkloric, yet modern.

He never saw her again. And to this day, hard as he might try, he can not remember an iota of whatever happened to Priday and his date that prom night when he used him as an excuse to satisfy his (Priday's) concupiscence, his lustful teenage loins.

The only thing he remembers clearly of the actual prom itself was that he bought her a lavender corsage which reminded him of that corny song of which the only thing he liked was its title: "Lavender Blue." They both trembled at his pinning the orchid above her left breast. They must have driven home that night to end the date, but he has no memory of her at all after that night she came out of the Cliff House. They must have said goodnight but he does not remember if he kissed her or not, nothing, that unmentionable, for some, that dreaded moment, the prize of the prom—that goodnight kiss. No memory of it at all. Just the ocean, the beach, the moon, the wind, the Cliff House, the steaming smell of hot dogs, burnt cotton candies, and Playland by the Sea that disappeared into the mist and recesses of San Francisco history, but not from memory, at least not from his.

First published in *Tayo Literary Magazine*, Issue 4, December 22, 2013,
www.tayoliterarymag.com

INITIATION:
MY FILIPINO TATTOO EXPERIENCE

Felicia Perez

Tattoos have always fascinated me. I remember sitting on my Uncle Lapu Lapu's lap as a child, giggling and laughing as I touched the picture of a scantily clothed woman on his arm, a tattoo he received while in the army during the Korean War. As I grew older, my attention was captured by the intricate designs on the skin of strangers, friends and family. These "symbols" carried the essence, archetypes and soul of the individual, a skin journal of the self. Yet even with my avid interest in tattoos, I felt hesitant to receive one myself. I couldn't imagine myself sitting in a tattoo shop, hearing the drilling sounds of the machine with rave music blasting, while a man covered in tattoos and piercings, went about tattooing something "meaningful and sacred" on my body. I knew on an intuitive level that spirituality and tattooing went hand in hand, something that could be found in my Filipino ancestry, but was lost to most Westerners.

As a teenager, I remember distinctly, as if my unconscious mind wanted me to carry the images and auditory sensations throughout time, a film I watched with my parents called *The Bounty*. The film was based upon a historical event of an English crew during the 1700s that mutinied against their captain in the Tahitian islands. Mel Gibson played the leader of the mutiny named Fletcher Christian. There is a scene in the film where Fletcher receives a traditional Tahitian hand-tapped tattoo in the hut of the local chieftain's daughter. His Tahitian lover is comforting him by massaging his head as women are chanting in the background. His face looks intense, yet peaceful as if he is receiving a sacrament. The sound of the tapping echoes throughout my mind.

I often "forget" my Filipino ancestors as I become unconscious and develop amnesia from the stresses of the modern world, where the mind and ego rule and intuition and spirit go underground. The ancestors are always present in between the world of spirit and this physical plane. They do not want to be forgotten, so they send messages and signs that serve to wake me up, often in dreams, but many times through individuals I feel connected to spiritually. I received one of these wake up calls in an email I received from my friend Leny Strobel about the agenda for the Center for Babaylan Studies (CFBS) weekend retreat held at her home in Northern California. In her email, she mentioned that Philippine tattoo expert Lane Wilcken would also be giving hand-tapped tattoos—an ancient Filipino style of tattooing using a boar's tusk and wild orange thorns. I felt a rush of excitement and without needing to think about it, immediately responded, "I want a hand-tapped tattoo!"

When I first arrived at the retreat, I felt an immediate sense of comfort, a homecoming with kindred spirits meeting collectively as if we had prearranged this meeting thousands of years ago. There was much food, laughter and indigenous Filipino music playing. I could feel that our intentions were pure, sacred and purposeful. I had no idea when I would receive my tattoo, until it was revealed during our circle of sharing that it would be witnessed by the entire group while we told stories of our ancestral tribal myths and folktales. I took a deep breath, knowing at that moment that what I was about to experience would be transformative, beyond my reasoning capacity, beyond the self.

For the tattoo design, I had chosen an image of the sun to be placed on the right side of my back. According to Lane Wilcken, the right side represents my father's Filipino ancestral lineage. I asked Lane to base the design on a

Felicia Perez

16th century illustration of a Visayan man covered in tattoos, which was drawn by a Spanish colonizer in a manuscript known as "The Boxer Codex." The pre-colonial *babaylans* (Filipino healers) had also honored the sun in their rituals with dance and music. I couldn't fully grasp it at the time, but I knew there was hidden wisdom in the sun. I now believe my Filipino ancestors were privy to this knowledge.

> *Tapping, Tapping*
> *Ink on skin*
> *Awakens memories from within*

The first tap of the orange thorn hit my back with intense force as the sound reverberated within my ears, like sonar waves it opened a gateway into a spiritual realm. I immediately saw myself in a cave with a Filipino man dressed in pre-colonial clothing. His red *putong* on his head stood out as he kneeled, looking directly at me as I received the tattoo. He appeared to be related to me genetically, an ancestor watching over my initiation into the deeper mysteries of life. As Lane continued tapping, my ancestor's image slowly began to disappear. I felt like I was somewhere between a waking state and a dream state of consciousness.

The sound of the tapping, like drums used by shamans in indigenous cultures, lulled me into a trance. With the *kulintang a kayo* (wooden kulintang) playing softly in the background, I felt the comfort of Will and Lorial tending gracefully to the wounds on my back. I felt the gentle touches of more friends, of Titania's hands as she rubbed my cold feet and Marybelle as she massaged my lower back with her cat-like fingers.

I could hear the group talking about their myths and stories, but from a distance and in muffled voices, yet they were right next to me. I only remember pieces of the stories. The pain, struggles and strength of individual and archetypal experiences sunk within me as each tap of ink entered into my skin. I heard the voices of our ancestors in the voices of the storytellers next to me: Will, Lizae, Catherine, Marybelle, Lorial, Titania, Joanna, Roque and Leny. Each one spoke "truth" that had been buried in order to adapt to the surrounding culture, a culture which doesn't hold space for grief, connection and wholeness.

I felt something emerging within me, like a dolphin swimming to the surface of the ocean to breathe or lava flowing at a steady pace down a hill. There was a rising sensation flowing through me as I held my trance for four hours during the tattoo ritual. I felt what was being "birthed" within me was ancient wisdom resurfacing from the past and into the present. It had to be rekindled through indigenous ritual, community, truth telling, emotional connectedness and spiritual aliveness. This type of wisdom cannot be learned through books and Western schooling. It needed to be "experienced" by letting go of the ego or mind and reconnecting with spirit.

What I learned was that the sun design on my back was not just an inanimate object in the universe. It was not just something that took up space or could be described only in scientific terms as a depiction of a star which emanates light and expends its energy resulting in life on earth. What was revealed to me was this: my Filipino ancestors knew that the sun was conscious of itself!

I will forever treasure my Filipino hand-tapped tattoo experience. I feel honored and blessed that I was given the privilege to be a part of something so sacred and ethereal. This story will be passed down to all my descendants, as I now know that I will be present, as an ancestor, during their own Philippine tattoo initiations.

SAKADA

Robert V. Ragsac, Sr.

We left our *barangay* just boys so young
Eager to start a daring adventure
A contract necklace for each boy was hung
That showed the new *Sakada*'s indenture

We said our goodbyes maybe forever
Starting life with but few pesos in hand
The moment to leave was now or never
Not sure when we'll return to our homeland

From the barangay the Ilokanos came
Rode Manila-bound trucks, away for good
Different barangay but Iloko all same
Each had come to find his livelihood

The Philippine Islands drifted away
From so many hardships we all did flee
We were all so sure that this was the way
To fortune in the islands Hawai'i

We're lowly passengers in ship's steerage
Crowded, with so many strange sounds and smells
We talk of family and heritage
Listening to the rolling ship's groans and bells

Robert V. Ragsac, Sr.

The Philippine Islands drifted away
From so many hardships we all did flee
We were all so sure that this was the way
To fortune in the islands Hawai'i

The island O'hau some could say
Was our Ellis Island of Hawai'i
And claim that Aloha Tower should play
For or us as the Statue of Liberty

Maybe they were signs of liberation
And a happy future we were to live
On Hawai'i Sugar Cane Plantation
Earning riches this island was to give

Hawai'i Sugarcane Planters Association
Was the only way we thought with eager youthful pride
Would earn our fortune in the sugar cane plantation
Opportunity the Philippines couldn't provide

We work endless acres of sugar cane
Tall waving stalks so coarse, then cut and burned
We chop by hand then load the cane haul train
Hard stoop labor for meager dollars earned

Field work is hard and the owners more so
From dawn to dusk, tomorrow is today
The smell of sugar cane as we all know
Means so much profit for H.S.P.A

Robert V. Ragsac, Sr.

Is this the promised work that would earn us
The money that would make our dreams come true?
But now it's hard labor monotonous
Would we be *Sakada* if we then knew?

We needed a fair, decent living wage
So asked to meet for negotiation
But demands were strongly met with outrage
And swift force that crushed all opposition

It's not our nature to go out and strike
But H.S.P.A. would soon realize
That it will not matter what they would like
Manlapit would lead us to organize

Many times at night we would all wonder
As we sing sentimental songs of home
If being Sakada was a blunder
When we're so tired and ache to the bone

In quiet nights old stories we'd retell
Of a cute *Pinay*'s love, her arms longed for
Or family life remembered so well
Until the longing we could stand no more

Lucky we talked story with a preacher
Who helped us face the loneliness
His *asawa* who became our teacher
Gave us much needed hope and happiness

Robert V. Ragsac, Sr.

Both helped us to overcome and endure
And softened the sting of lonely despair
Lifted our spirits to grasp the future
Lightened the burden that we had to bear

Quietly counseled our fears, soothed heartaches
Helping sakadas was their sole mission
They taught us to read and write for our sakes
Dios ti agngina Manong/Manang Dizon

All sakadas looked after each other
Talked many stories of their barangay
So any who's a friend became "Brother"
Kabsat always till the last breath we sigh

Dreary *campo* life, little time to play
Living together bunched in small cabins
Being exploited, hard work, meager pay
Work sunrise to sunset callused our brains

Talking story while working soothes the pain
Fields of cane to chop, pineapples to pick
Today was yesterday, try to stay sane
Sweat we did, but can't afford to get sick

For some sakadas their hard work would end
Paid to return home, many of us did
Others' lives on plantation they would spend
But many heard that new adventures bid

Robert V. Ragsac, Sr.

The Mainland promised a much better life
And renewed old dreams of a life so grand
We left the plantation and labor strife
Hoping to be more than just a field hand

But pineapples became grapes and lettuce
Growers powerful as H.S.P.A.
Sugar cane turned into asparagus
Then the Great Depression forced us to stay

Anti-Filipino gangs we endured
Denied citizenship, made life a cage
Organize for improvements we're assured
As before our demands brought racial rage

Our youthful hopes grew dim, but not the love
And with hardened hearts we all knew we can
Overcome prejudice and rise above
And be proud citizens American

Sakada no more, some marry, have children
Who are the first Fil-Am generation
But some older *Pinoys* bear a burden
As single *manongs* of our migration

Now those *Manongs'* voices are heard no more
Many dreams did die and hope surrendered
This *Pinoy* First Wave to break on this shore
But will their life stories be remembered?

NANA MENG'S TSOKOLATE

Marivic Reyes-Restivo

"*M*ang, can you send me a bottle of Nana Meng's *Tsokolate?*"
This is how my conversation starts when I talk to my mom who resides in Manila. It starts with a request for a taste I crave, something comforting and familiar that echoes of childhood visits to Santa Maria, the town where my parents are from and the locale of the Reyes ancestral home. This is what the brutal New York winters and the impending holidays do to me. It makes me homesick and envious of family members who have vacationed there more often than I.

"You can send it through Ben, Mang." "*At ikaw? Kailan ka uuwi?*"*

"I don't know Mang. Maybe soon." The half truth issues from my lips knowing fully well that visits will may likely mean a couple of years or more. The lackluster economy has made it harder to fly home on a semi-regular basis.

Silence. It's a drawn-out one. The unspoken words carry more weight than the ones articulated—my mom's vulnerability at age eighty-eight and all the limitations it bears. The same woman once towered over me and offered "advice" long after I married and bore a son. She has shrunken to my height after osteoporosis claimed her bones. I also know in her eyes that somehow I've finally gotten things right. My feelings run deep—the regret of an only daughter unable to fulfill her fragile mother's immediate wish.

After ending the call, I get the urge again to cook something Filipino. Admittedly, married to an Italian has put the native cuisine on the back-

---

**And when will you go home?*

burner. Forty plus years of living in this melting pot has also influenced my taste buds, making Filipino dishes far and few.

I make a quick run to the local Japanese store for the glutinous rice and the nearby Stop and Shop for the coconut milk and cream in the Asian food aisle. Within the hour, I am at my stove, carefully stirring the rice in the coconut milk as if making risotto. I add the brown sugar, which turns the mixture to a soft caramel color. I hear Mang's voice in my head not to overcook the rice. "It's good to leave some firmness to it," she would've said had she been standing by my side, like she did when I was young and first learning to cook from her. I pour the *biko* mixture into a pan and smother it with the sweetened coconut cream. She would've been proud of my handiwork.

And so it goes on for weeks. More Filipino dishes emerge from my American kitchen. Instead of pasta, I make *pansit*, rice noodles in a medley of vegetables and pork.

Instead of chicken noodle soup, I make *nilaga*, beef shank that's been molten in its broth, with chickpeas and cabbage. The favorite roast chicken is replaced with the ever reliable adobo in all its different variations.

The longing that started with a gentle stir has now built into a tug I can no longer ignore. I am reminded of the years that have passed since my last visit. Memories pile up like snow banks on the sidewalks of Port Washington—tree limbs heavy from the weight of them.

Curled up and blanketed on my sofa, I recall the aromas of a weekday morning in the old ancestral home. The smell of hot *tsokolate* permeating the morning air, and the sound of a *batidor* beating against the aluminum pot, creating foam in the rich brown liquid. Nana Meng, Dad's older sister, is in the kitchen holding court among the cooks and the *kasama*, farmer tenants who've worked our land from one generation to the next. There is a huge breakfast spread on the table. Hot *pandesal* rolls compete for space with the Anchor butter and pillows of *quesong puti*, farmer's cheese still warm and wrapped in banana leaves. There is garlic fried rice, beef *tapa*, fried eggs, and canned sardines that have been sauteed in onions and its own tomato sauce. There is *lacatan*, the proverbial banana, to polish off one's meal.

Nana Meng has already been up since 5:30 A.M., gone to mass, shopped at the wet market, and reviewed the menu with the cooks. The *sari sari* convenience store, which is attached to the ancestral home, has been opened for business since 6:30 A.M. From the kitchen you can hear a shopper call out loud, "*tao po*," signifying his or her presence and the need for help with groceries.

Nana Meng's round face is powdered and there is a trace of lipstick on her lips. Her indispensable pastel colored frames lie low on her nose. She pulls out her laced hanky to wipe the beads of perspiration on her forehead.

Ka Elo, the head farmer, and group spokesperson, has dropped by. His skin's been browned and wrinkled by the sun. His hair is jet black belying his years. One of his front teeth is capped in gold and there are several teeth missing on the sides. His silent companions are happy to let him talk while they dig into their meal. One of them, the younger skinnier one, spears the beef *tapa* with his fork.

"*Mga dalawang kaing ang dadalin ko sa palengke. At isang kaing dito.*"

Ka Elo explains how the harvest of mangoes will be split. Two will be delivered to the public market for sale while one will be delivered to Nana Meng for family consumption.

I can only imagine the fragrant scent of ripening mangoes nestled in burlap, and the honeyed taste exploding in my mouth, juices dripping. The thought of them makes me hunger for more. Not the kind I get in the local grocery stores but the ones only found at home.

The stir that became a tug has now evolved into a pang. I feel the need to be adrift in a sea of brown faces not unlike my own. To walk the familiar narrow paths lined with shabby storefronts and more people than it can own.

To listen to the mass in a language I can barely follow and a visit to the stone cemetery of ancestors long gone. I miss the riot of crowds and color and honking and noise. My heart tells me it's time to make a trip home.

I do not know if my attachment to Santa Maria will be as strong once my mother is gone, but this is what I know for now. With each visit to the ancestral home, I notice slight changes. The gatherings are less frequent and not everyone attends. There are so many aunts and uncles that have been long gone. My grandmother, on my dad's side, is the only one of her generation living. But there is a large part of me that is unwilling to give up my space there nor my memories. So for now, I will also call Santa Maria my home. Home is where I want it to be—it is both in the arms of my birthplace and in the warm embrace of my adoptive country.

RECIPE FOR NANA MENG'S TSOKOLATE

Boil 2 cups of water.
Stir in 3 tablespoons of Nana Meng's Tsokolate until well dissolved.
Add ¼ cup full cream or evaporated milk plus 3 tablespoons sugar.
Stir until well blended.
Makes 3-4 cups.

Nana Meng's Tsokolate is my aunt's personal blend of peanuts and cacao, ground and turned into a paste for hot chocolate. It is a recipe my niece borrowed, bottled and labeled in her honor. It is currently sold at the *tiangges*, the public markets of Manila.

UP AND DOWN

Tony Robles

Manang Gerarda comes into
my office pushing one of
those metal walkers with wheels that drag
across concrete

she sits down and
tells me about her
doctor's visit

I look at her hands, her
fingers are thick and
gnarled and I wouldn't
want them around my
neck

I help her fill out forms
for housing, healthcare
and other things

Gerarda speaks to me in
English but then
she'll suddenly break
into Pilipino and she
thinks I understand

Tony Robles

I sit and shake my
head and her voice sounds
like rainwater on the softness
of rocks which I understand

Manang Gerarda, living in a
senior residence and sending
money back home
to fund a school she started
back in the PI

Manang Gerarda, bringing
bags of food that she gets
from the nearby food
pantry because she thinks
I don't eat

we walk down the street
together and she takes
ahold of my arm

She is so strong
she could pull the
bark off a palm tree

She walks on bow legs
and her body sways from
side to side

Tony Robles

Her eyes drift as we
walk past trees playing
hide and seek with
children

I ask her what
kind of work she
did years ago

and she smiles
and says, up
and down, up
and down

she says she was
an elevator operator
in a high-class hotel

Said she was in
good with the hotel
owner who once paid
her way to New York

She stayed in a
luxury suite
lobster, wine
the whole nine

Tony Robles

I look at her legs
and back and face
and a smile breaks through
the silence

I live an up
and down
life she says

Her eyes
lifting into
mine

STIRRED

Michele Santos-Gutierrez

The year my father filed for divorce, my mother joined the Sacred Heart prayer group, a collection of about two-dozen Filipino women from the local Catholic Church who would take turns hosting a toddler-sized statue of an adult Jesus at their altars at home. Whoever was keeping the statue would host that week's prayer sessions in honor of Jesus, the Sacred Heart.

I was eight years old when I attended my first vigil with my mother. After praying the Rosary, Magdalena, the leader of the group, stood with her eyes closed as the rest of us sat cross-legged on the floor watching her.

"Our father, who art in heaven," she began. As she looked up to the ceiling, her eyes began to flicker, and her speech grew faster until her words were barely recognizable. Suddenly, they became clear again, taking on a lower register, as if she were trying to imitate a large man.

"I am the lord your God, there is no other God except me."

Magdalena approached the first woman, who rose from her seated position on the floor to kneel.

"What is your name my child?" the deep voice asked the woman.

"I am Betty."

With her hand on Betty's forehead, Magdalena spoke in a deeper voice, but I could no longer make out anything that she was saying. She moved Betty's head, first in little circles and then bigger ones until, eventually, Betty's entire body was swaying in an orbit around her center. Betty spun and spun, and Magdalena's voice grew deeper and faster until the woman fell. Another woman positioned a pillow underneath Betty to catch her plummeting head.

Betty laid on the floor motionless, with her eyes closed as Magdalena moved on to the next woman, and then to a boy and a girl, repeating the ritual more than a dozen times. I closed my eyes as Magdalena planted her hand to my own forehead and stirred the rest of me, slow at first, and then faster and faster, in larger circles as if I were a giant wooden ladle and she was stirring me in a cauldron of hot water.

Should I feel something? I wondered. Did everyone else feel something? Or did everyone else just pretend to feel something, because they thought everyone else was feeling something? I wrinkled my forehead and tried to pray, but I was too distracted by the spinning, and the fact that nothing was happening to me.

Magdalena moved me more violently as my turn took longer than expected. The others joined her, chanting and praying, not in tongues, but with the familiar words and rhythm of the Our Father. I felt sick and dizzy. Thinking I might throw up, I decided to fall. I made my body limp and heavy, and aimed my head in one controlled motion towards the pillow I trusted was behind me. Those who had yet to take their turns, and those who had already awoken from their own spells celebrated with cheers as my body hit the ground. I joined the others who were still on the floor with their eyes closed. I pretended I was one of them. I laid there listening. When it was my mother's turn, I listened to her collapse to the floor, taking only a fraction of the time it had taken me.

My mother transformed our fireplace into an elaborate altar. It held three different versions of the *Santo Niño*, and a portrait of Jesus with a crown of thorns around its battery powered heart—a heart that I could see even on the blackest of nights because it glowed in the dark and illuminated Jesus' sad eyes. There were dozens of statues of saints too, such as St. Anthony—patron saint of missing people, St. Epipodius—patron saint of those who have been betrayed and tortured, and St. Lucy—patron saint of the blind.

Out of all of them, my mother took the greatest care of her porcelain Virgin Mary. She was two feet high, dressed in white from head to toe, and as my mother claimed, cried when no one was looking.

Just like me.

We lived in the three-bedroom house my father left behind. It had two empty bedrooms, but I shared my mother's room and the other half of her queen-sized bed, even as I grew nearly queen-sized myself. I knew there was a man-sized hole in my mother's heart, and it was a hole I could never fill, no matter how much she tried to fit me into it.

The last time my father tried to pick me up for our court-appointed weekend visits, I was nine years old. I sat at the top of the stairs, listening.

"*Anak*, open the door. I want to see you. Open the door, please," he pleaded.

"He doesn't love you," my mother told me, "If he did, he would try harder to see you."

I sat on the stairs and I didn't even try to open the door.

"Do you want to see your father?" my mother asked me.

I did, but I told her no.

"Good, because I don't know what I would do if you left me," she said, "I would die. Do you want me to die?"

I looked at her and said nothing. Instead, I listened to my father begging me to open the door. I wanted him to take an axe and tear down the door, but instead, he came back with a police officer to try to get to me.

"Ma'am, your husband wants to see your child," the police officer said.

"He's not my husband."

"Your ex-husband then. He has a legal right to see her."

My mother called me to the door. "Do you want to go with your father?" she asked me. I looked at my father through the holes in the metal door.

I didn't answer my mother. I simply cried.

"It's probably best for your daughter if you just let her be," the police officer told my father, "You don't want this to be harder for her."

My father stopped showing up for our visits, and my mother prayed and prayed. She asked baby Jesus, and the Virgin Mary, and her entire army of holy figures to intercede on our behalf so that my father would come back to us. I would kneel next to her as she recited the *Our Father* or *Hail Mary* over and over again, the callouses on my knees growing thicker each day.

My mother always held a prayer under her breath. Whispering. Always whispering.

>*Our Father, who art in heaven*
>*Hallowed be thy name*

She would stand in front of the stove, cooking me *sinigang* or chicken with green beans.

>*Thy kingdom come*
>*Thy will be done*
>*On earth as it is in heaven*

Watching TV, her eyes glazed over.

>*Give us this day our daily bread*
>*And forgive us our trespasses*

Fighting sleep, her hand propping up her head at her temples.

>*As we forgive those who trespass against us*
>*And lead us not into temptation*

Angry. Hitting and slapping me, praying the whole time as I fought back.

>*But deliver us from evil*

I'd watch her hold her right hand to her heart, clasping her fist closed as if holding a worn rosary that wasn't there.

>*Amen.*

The day I realized I was bigger and stronger than my mother, I told her, "He's not coming back, Mom. Let it go."

"You're just like your dad," she screamed, "*Leche ka!* Go to him if you love him so much!"

She slapped me, and I pushed her back like so many times before, except this time, she fell, hard on the floor. Looking down at her, I decided it was better if I stopped using my fists to fight back.

I attended my last vigil with my mother. When it was my turn to be spun, I knelt in front of Magdalena. I closed my eyes as she stirred me around my own center, in her familiar way—slow small circles, and then increasingly in faster, larger ones. She stirred and stirred and stirred, but I still did not fall. I did not pretend to sleep.

Magdalena's voice grew deeper and the rest of the members of the Sacred Heart prayer group joined in, but I still did not fall. I became a kid-sized statue. I opened my eyes and stiffened my body enough so that Magdalena could no longer move me. There was a small commotion among the others, and for a moment, Magdalena fell out of character.

"What are you doing?" she asked me in her regular voice.

Everyone fell silent. I said nothing. I simply rose up, and went to the kitchen, listening while my mother took her own turn at falling.

In silence, we drove home, where I moved all my clothes and things out of my mother's room and transferred them to the empty drawers in one of our extra bedrooms.

"What are you doing?" my mother asked me.

I did not answer her. Instead, I got up from my own bed, closed the door, and locked it from the inside.

SNIPPETS OF GRANDPA'S SIMPLE LIFE IN AMERICA

Lourdes Sobredo

He was 90 years old, frail and visibly shrunken in his old age. That's how I remember him before he passed away. He liked listing his height on his driver's license as 5 feet and 3 inches. I just smiled inside but never called him on it. And watching him in his bed, he looked even shorter than the 5 feet that he really was when he could still drive. When I leaned over to touch his forehead, I'd see his eyes glued to my movement until we locked glances right before I kissed his head. I was leaving for a three-day business conference in San Diego and little did I know, that was the last time I would see him alive.

The morning following my return home from the trip, I got dressed and prepared to visit Grandpa at the convalescent home in Stockton, California where he spent the last two years of his life. A phone call from the nurse on duty changed my plans. It was no longer to visit Grandpa to share stories. It was to arrange for his funeral, and to fulfill the promise to see him after my conference. He died minutes before that morning phone call on Saturday, November 4, 1995. He looked peaceful in his eternal state of sleep. Many images and snippets of his life were racing in my mind's eye. As I said my goodbye and trying very hard to hold back the tears, I thanked him for my life and time with him, with my grandpa, my *Lolo* Olong. I was 42 years old.

Grandpa was my maternal grandfather. He was Lolo Olong to me and to his family and close friends. He was Perfecto Torcuator de los Santos on his baptismal certificate and California driver's license, and Pet to some of his friends and acquaintances in California. He was born in Cayangwan, Makato (a farming village) in the province of Aklan within the island of Panay in the Western Visayas of the Philippines. I vaguely recall my mother telling me that her father's true date of birth was November 3, 1904, not March 3, 1905 as his papers may have stated when he arrived in Seattle, Washington in 1929. So in reality, he died at 91, not 90 as his death record showed. He worked most of his life as a farm worker in the San Joaquin and Salinas Valleys of California and in the Alaskan fish canaries in the off-season. For me, as a granddaughter of a Filipino farm worker in California and an *Alaskero*, eating steamed asparagus and boiled salmon heads is like paying homage to the blood, sweat, tears and sacrifices of my elder. Savoring asparagus at family mealtime invariably came with some commentary from a family member, usually me, about how asparagus helped finance my mother's education.

The repertoire of dishes my grandfather cooked was ordinary. And so I thought until I invited a Jewish American friend to dinner. I purposely prepared a typical American meal, although I don't clearly remember now what that consisted. It did not take long for my friend to notice that Grandpa was eating a totally different dish. The aroma was inescapably different from the food she and I were eating. She asked what it was. When she found out it was calamari cooked in its dark ink simmered in vinegar and many cloves of garlic, she told him that was her favorite and asked to try it. She was impressed. Grandpa grinned from ear to ear with pride as his *adobong pusit* became the dish of choice. That evening earned Lolo Olong gold stars from my friend for his cooking. But the comfort food I remember most from dishes Lolo Olong prepared was what he called *campo* muffin, something he learned to make as a cook for many years in the farm workers' camp where he lived during harvest season in California. I called it comfort food, not because it was comfortable to the taste—I used to wonder why the muffins were so huge and hard to swallow. It was comfort food because he thoroughly enjoyed baking them for my cousins and me well into his 70s and 80s. Those are the same cousins who relished the taste of this muffin and thought me too harsh in my critique. Lolo had this impish grin while he dunked the muffin in his cup of coffee. Wishing now that I had asked what memories were running through him whenever he re-enacted this ritual often. Indeed, I found comfort in knowing he made them with his hands full of love. I would share this snapshot about my *lolo*'s cooking to friends and they would ask, "How compact was this muffin anyway?" Let's just say, after a day or two, you could toss it against a wall and it wouldn't fall apart. Maybe I am exaggerating, but the memory conjures up an image of a grandfather who made do with what little he had and he remained both humble in heart and stubborn in his opinion well into his old age.

Stubborn, I said? At age 74, he wanted to renew his driver's license. Driving was what Grandpa did whenever he could in his old, blue-green Ford Falcon, mostly to play cards at the Iloilo Circle or buy a pair of pants and hat at Marianni's Department Store on El Dorado Street in Stockton. By the time he retired from farm work, I was in high school. He mostly drove to take me to school, help my mom with her grocery shopping or play rummy with his friends. As long as he could drive, he was happy. On the other hand, family was not too keen on him continuing to drive as he was showing signs of forgetting the route to get home from the grocery store. He blamed it on the new neighborhood. But he wanted to renew his driver's license and no one could persuade him otherwise. Oh, he seriously studied for the written test. I even drove him to the office of the Department of Motor Vehicles (DMV). He passed with flying colors until he was required to take a driving test. How did he do? He didn't. He couldn't even get the car started. Maybe I shouldn't have done this…I drove him in a new car he had never driven before, and he wasn't familiar with the instrument panel. He was so embarrassed and mad about the experience, he didn't want to go back to take the test again. I vividly recall how he mumbled softly yet angrily in his Aklanon language and scratched and shook his mostly bald head to show his displeasure. I always thought that he eventually forgave me for tricking him into flunking his driving test.

Lolo had very little possessions. It must have been part of the migrant farm worker/*Alaskero*'s life-on-the-go. I remember a time he was packing to take a trip, I think his last, to work in Alaska. He was in his mid-60's. The thick, dark grey wool blanket, the dark green and black wool plaid jacket, the brown leather shaving kit, grey hat, and the small tanned valise were a common site on these departures. The shaving kit is still with me. And the grey hat, too. Regretfully, I kept nothing more than that. I really didn't know how much discrimination he encountered over the years. Even with his tendency to be opinionated about many things, he did not speak of any. He did not complain. He would occasionally reminisce about the Japanese American family who helped him during the Great Depression, but the details were scanty. He was happiest while in the company of his *kababayan* or town mates from the Philippines. And when he outlived most of them, he would lament how they all left him. This was the feeling of isolation, of growing old and what living in America felt like to him. I fully appreciated those words when he, too, left this earth.

The convalescent home, operated by Filipinos, with mostly Filipino nurses and staff did their best to make residents like Lolo engaged in activities. I visited often. Because I worked nearby at the time, I sometimes joined him for lunch and dinner. I could still picture the biggest smile from him when he saw his first and only great-grandchild. He was 89 and Sonny was 4 months old. He was ecstatic to have lived long enough to meet his descendant. He could not take his eyes off my son. I choked back the tears, grateful that he was able to hold my son's fingers in his lifetime, yet deeply pained that his daughter, my mother died too young to participate in the moment. I imagined he, too, felt the same.

The plant life he harvested while working in the farms in his youth put food on the table and supported my grandmother who died at a much younger age than he did. He also managed to send his only daughter to college, but never managed to return home to the Philippines. Not being able to physically work the farms anymore meant he no longer had to wake up early in the dark and chilly mornings. But routines were hard to break, or maybe rising before the break of dawn was part and parcel to growing older. He still woke up at 4:00 A.M., slightly later than his typical farm worker days. He made hot coffee, that meant boiled hot water and Instant Folger's coffee, and guess what else? Those muffins from the *"campo."* Years before the convalescent home, he managed to turn my family backyard into a small farm. Riled with colors of summer and at harvest time, various shapes of vegetables essential to Filipino cooking, he marveled at his own garden. He would irrigate the plots of vegetables and inspect each with the utmost of care. He would stand at the patio for hours as if attending to a greater-than-life farm of his own. I think he was most at peace in the garden. When the limitations of old age kept him from attending to his garden, the plants slowly shriveled away while his eyes full of melancholy could only watch them through his bedroom window. The juxtaposition of those two images was not lost to me. And I venture to guess, not to him either. I so appreciated and loved this frail and visibly diminutive old man saying his slow goodbye to the plant life outside his window, saying goodbye to his simple life in America. He was my Grandpa, my *Lolo* Olong.

A LIFE FORGOTTEN

Monica Valerio

Five times per week, I visit my mother's home, and climb the ten steps into her house. I stand next to her bed, and ask her the same question, hoping against all odds that I'll have a different answer. Unfortunately, the answer is always the same.

"Mom, do you know who I am?" She'll look into my eyes with very faint recognition, yet no names come to her mind.

"No, I don't know who you are."

"It's your daughter, Monica, and I'm here to change you."

Most times, Mom will comply, but once in awhile she'll verbally argue with me, still unsure of who I am, and I calmly put her at ease, so she won't feel threatened by the presence of this "unknown stranger."

Ten years ago, Mom was diagnosed with Alzheimer's. The doctor let us know that her condition would get worse over time. Two years ago, she suffered a stroke and is completely bedridden. She can no longer walk or feed herself.

I, along with five brothers and sisters, my mother's two sisters (Helen and Angie), and an older Filipino couple (Tirso and Minay) who rent a room in my mother's home, all participate in the care of my mother. Confining her to a rest home was out of the question. In many cultures, the children assume responsibility for care of their aging parents. This holds true among many Filipino families. We knew that between us, we could give her the care that she needed. We stopped charging Tirso and Minay rent when they began helping with the care of my mother. Between the six of us siblings, we worked out a schedule where we could fill in the gaps for the care of my mom.

Monica Valerio

The other siblings did duties such as home repairs, yard work and buying supplies.

With each passing day, I am grateful to still have my mother. After all, she is still the woman who used to sew dresses for me, and cook my favorite Filipino foods that I still cannot duplicate even to this day. She is still the woman who managed to raise 12 children by herself, after my father passed away in 1969, which made her a widow at the young age of 44. At the time she was widowed, there were still 11 children living at home. My mom never had to work until my father got very ill. It was only then that she went to Beauty School to learn a trade, and become a beautician, eventually opening up her own beauty shop. She was never seen as the disciplinarian. In my opinion, I saw us as "self-managing." It amazes me that none of us ever got into serious trouble during our childhood and teenage years.

My mother is the woman who delivered my daughter 34 years ago, in her bedroom, because I did not know I was in labor. I am convinced that my daughter, Bonnie, shares a special bond with her grandmother because of that delivery. My mom helped me buy the house I am living in, which is located directly behind her 125-year-old Victorian home. With us living so close, Mom was able to lavish a lot of attention on Bonnie throughout her childhood and teenage years. How I miss the times of my one-on-one conversations with Mom, when she talked about her life, as well as the struggles she endured in the 1940s. I remember her story of the discrimination she encountered when she tried to buy her first home in Alameda. Homes were "no longer for sale" when she looked at the properties. After she was turned down three times, she purchased her first home sight unseen, using only a home description and price to base her buying decision.

Every year, major holidays are still celebrated in her home, a tradition that started when we were young. On Easter, Thanksgiving and Christmas, we head over to Mom's house for our potluck lunch. Having lunch meals together left my brothers and sisters free to celebrate the evening meals with their spouse's family. With seven brothers and four sisters, it is rare when all 12 of us are present during any one of the holidays.

Mom does not recognize the faces of her own children or grandchildren, or the variety of relatives who pop into her bedroom to greet her. Names will be familiar, once we remind her who we are. Although we always have to tell her who we are each and every time we see her, I don't believe she remembers anything about us, but she acts like she does. Anytime we tell her "I love you," she would always respond, "I love you, too."

Alzheimer's has robbed her of her once active mind, and she'll lay awake at night singing aloud for hours and hours at a time, or having conversations with people we cannot see or hear. Oftentimes, her reality is a past that existed some 70+ years ago, when she lived as a child in Kauai, Hawaii, and as a teenager in Luzon, Philippines, before coming to Alameda as a war bride in 1946. She remembers little of the very full life she once led, or raising her children as a single parent. She'll often ask us to take her "home" (meaning the Philippines), because she says her mother will be worried about her. In her mind, she is that young teenager with a very strict mother.

My brother Alex, the eldest of the siblings, told us the following story about Mom:

> "One day she was looking down and moving her hands. I asked her what she was doing. She said she was dancing. I asked her 'Where are you?' She said she was in school. Mom ended up describing in detail her plantation school in Hawaii, the sugar cane fields outside, and the dirt road."

Sometimes, Mom will speak to us in her native language, although I (as well as all of my brothers and sisters) never learned the language and understand very little of her native tongue. Fortunately, Mom's sisters and Tirso and Minay speak to her in her native language, which give my mom great comfort.

CONCLUSION:
Two months after this story was written (and presented by me at my Toastmasters Meeting), my mother passed away. She died on November 17, 2010, two days after her 86th birthday. On the evening of her birthday, Mom's three sisters, Tirso and Minay, my sister Mary, my boyfriend Jerry and I surrounded her bed and sang "Happy Birthday." Although she did not know who we were, we all witnessed my mother singing in a barely audible voice, the last song she did remember—The "Happy Birthday" song!

At the memorial service held for my mom, several siblings shared their stories of my mother. One of the eulogies was given by my sister, Carmencita, who said the following:

> *"From speeches to programs found, I learned what an amazing woman my mother was, but because of her, I found out what an amazing family we were. She leaves a legacy of a family united, a family who worked together to take care of her."*

THE SOCIAL BOX

Jean Vengua

There was a period in my early teens when I went to Filipino community and club dances almost every weekend. On Thursdays my mother began baking pastries to sell in the dance hall. I helped out in the kitchen, rolling out the buttery yellow dough for *ensaimada* rolls and grating coconut for *palitaw*. On Fridays, we'd dress up–a big production; my mother and I really took the hair styling, makeup, and dressing-up seriously–and then we'd haul the two-gallon coffee makers and the Tupperware tubs full of pastries out to the car and drive off to pick up friends and head over to the dance, or what the Filipino teens of that era called the "Flip gig." If my father was home from his merchant marine job, he'd come along with his guitar and play in Mauro Ibarra's band. If he had shipped out, my mother and I would go with her friends to dances in Salinas, Sacramento, or San Francisco.

The Flip gigs were attended by a mix of kids, teens, middle-aged and old folks. Racially, the families were mixed: Filipino, white, Mexican, hapa, American Indian, Chinese, African-American. Women and girls might dance with male partners their age, but also with old–sometimes VERY old–*manongs*[1]. Women would dance with women, kids danced, nephews danced with aunties, and so on. Sometimes there would be two bands. The first band–the "old guys"–would play their set first, followed by a teen band, usually with a car name like the Thunderbirds or the Mustangs.

---

1. *Manong/manang*: terms used to refer to elders, male and female, respectively.

The social box would begin at around 11 P.M. Five to ten chairs were placed in front of the stage. Teenage girls and young women were chosen to come up front (*who* was chosen was no big deal; if you really wanted to do it, you could). One at a time, each had a turn to stand as the band played "Maria Elena." Then, one at a time, the men would come forward flashing bills, which were deposited in a cardboard box. Someone behind the microphone would announce the name of the donor and the amount: "TEN DOLLARS!" "TWENTY DOLLARS!" Sometimes it was more, $30 or $50. Each girl stayed on her feet as long as the money kept coming, 15 to 20 minutes at most.

Many who stepped up with money were old Filipino farmworkers spiffed up in suits that they'd bought in their heyday, during the 1930s. Still working in the fields—but getting too old to be doing that kind of hard labor—they'd left their harsh jobs behind for the weekend. At the dance, they were respected elder leaders of the local lodge, and they could relive their youth. Like my dad, many had worked in the Watsonville and Salinas areas during the anti-Filipino riots. Occasionally, a woman would step up and dance with a girl, smiling proudly, confident that she was maintaining her standing in the community. The ability to donate the money showed everyone that you were doing well, you could be generous.

I'd get half of my take from the social box, maybe $100 or more if I was lucky. The organization—usually the Caballeros de Dimas-Alang, Legionarios del Trabajo, or Filipino Community—would get the other half. In the 1960s, this wasn't bad pay for a 13 or 14-year-old. Some of my girlfriends worked in the fields and lived in labor camps; for them the social box take was important extra income for their family, and they'd have to give most or all of their money to their parents. My father's job on the ship was that of steward—essentially a valet. The pay was sufficient to pay our bills, but to be able to buy "nice things" for the house, my mother needed to get a job, and the social box money helped to buy my clothes. Although she had worked as a file clerk in a bank in the Philippines, the only job my mother could get in the U.S. was as a cannery worker.

The Birds Eye plant across the street from our house processed Brussels sprouts, and the stink of discarded sprouts in an open disposal pit outside Birds Eye wafted over the whole Westside neighborhood. The area was noisy, too. The sound of engines and squeal of brakes seemed nearly constant as trains stopped on the tracks near the cannery to pick up produce. Mom came home after every shift tired and smelling of Brussels sprouts. On her first day of work, the vegetables whizzing by on the conveyor belt made her dizzy and she nearly fainted. The floors in the cannery were routinely flooded with water that made her feet cold in their rubber boots, and it was hard to stand for hours at a time. She managed to stay on, somehow, and later was proud of how quickly she learned and how fast she was at sorting produce.

In high school, I kept silent about the social box. My white friends in the high school never had anything like this in their dances. And they would certainly never be caught dancing with some old guy. They went to dances and parties strictly for teens, preferably sans parents. I told only a few friends, usually Filipino or Mexican girls, or girls who, back then, were labeled "white trash" because, somehow, they understood. But that wasn't necessarily the case with their parents. Hearing about the social box, one friend was excited about the thought of making quick money and actually went to a dance with me and signed up. However, her mother soon showed up with two large men and quickly hustled her out of the dance hall.

By the time I participated in the social box, it had been an institution in Filipino communities for several decades. I don't know its origin among Filipinos in the U.S., but a book for teen readers published in 1918, *Jack and Janet in the Philippines*, mentions a "social box party" to raise money for a school in Bacolod: "The girls made boxes of *dulces* and sold them at auction, at an entertainment, to which the whole town was invited. The boys gave the coconuts and other materials for the *dulces*. One very popular girl's box brought six pesos."[2]

But by the mid-1960s, things were changing. Filipinos had drawn attention from the local press in the 1960s, and not always for good reasons. I ran for Dimas-Alang Lodge Queen in 1964, and there was a murder at my "tabulation" dance, a gang shooting. In tabulation dances raffle tickets were sold by the candidates and counted in order to figure out which of the competitors were ahead; they were important dances because they could bring in a lot of money. There was a certain excitement because social box contributors often made dramatically large contributions to show their support for a particular candidate. The shooting happened in the Portuguese Hall in Santa Cruz. I was thirteen years old. As I stood up for my turn in the social box, I heard what sounded like firecrackers. My mother suddenly grabbed my arm and pulled me into a back hallway. The brother of a friend of mine had appeared in the open entry of the dancehall, walked over to a young man seated at a bench against the wall, and fired several bullets into him. The victim died in the hospital the next day. I know that the newspapers ran the story, but nobody at my high school ever mentioned it to me, so isolated was our Filipino community from that of the mostly white, California beach community in which I lived.

Filipinos were also involved in labor disputes and protests at the time. One of my queen contest competitors from Delano couldn't always make it to dances, because she had to join the picket line during the grape pickers' strike. This strike began with a group of Filipino farmworkers led by Larry Itliong. But after they involved César Chávez and the United Farmworkers Union, the strike grew in size and intensity, drawing attention from the media and making real changes in the lives of the farmworkers. When the band

---

2. Thomas, Norma Waterbury. *Jack and Janet in the Philippines: A Sequel to Around the World with Jack and Janet*. (W. Medford, MA: The Central Committee of the United Study of Foreign Missions, 1918), 91

was on its break (the usual time for announcements made at the microphone), she would not only encourage people to buy raffle tickets, but also exhort them to join the protest.

I won the Queen contest for the Caballeros de Dimas-Alang in 1964. My mother and I drove to Los Angeles where I was crowned at a conference in the Hollywood Roosevelt Hotel. While I was proud of winning, I was also oddly resentful. We had a big blowup the night of the coronation over the color of my lipstick. I guess you could say that she was becoming sort of a "stage mother." She had my gown special-ordered and handmade in the Philippines. She herself had been elected the "1940 Muse of the Philippine Beauty and Fashion Carnival," and a few years later her younger sister held a similar title. It was a big deal, sort of like being the Queen of Mardi Gras, only whether or not you won depended mostly on the money you raised in ticket sales and your "sociability." Of course, being beautiful helped.

By the mid 1960s, some lodge members wanted to get rid of the social box. I often went with my mother to some of the lodge meetings, where I would sit in a corner and pretend to study; arguments about the social box were heated. "It's nothing but taxi dancing!" I remember someone saying. "*Walang-hiya!* It's shameful! Like prostitutes!" They wanted to invite local dignitaries to the dances, like mayors and council-members, to get their backing for scholarships and other projects. They were embarrassed to ask them over because of the social box.

There were also arguments about the Filipino queen contests, which were compared to queen contests viewed on American TV, where young, mostly white, women were paraded around in bathing suits, had to answer questions that supposedly proved their intelligence, and were awarded college scholarships. In contrast, winning a Filipino queen contest only because you could sell more tickets than any other girl seemed to reduce the winner to a mere question of numbers, rather than merit.

I remember feeling embarrassed, too, as if there was something shameful about it. Maybe this conflict justified my then-inexplicable anger at my mother when we fought in the Hollywood Roosevelt Hotel. I had won "only" because I sold more tickets than anyone else. I didn't think about the constant training in marketing myself and "social networking" that my mother put me through: the constant admonitions to get over my shyness and smile, make small talk, dress and speak well, and be polite with everyone, young or old, when I really would rather have sat in a corner reading a book. We even traveled to the labor camps, where we were invited to share meals with the field workers. There was a lot of talk, gossip, and news over bowls of steaming rice with *adobo* or fish head soup, and later we'd sell the workers tickets, securing their support for the next social box and queen contest tabulation.

The Filipino community clubs and lodges were split into factions for and against the social box and queen contests, although personality issues played a part, often reduced to conflicts about money or adultery. My mother and her friends and allies, mostly women, defended the social box with a surprising amount of passion, almost rage. They talked about it as if it was a lengthy and honored tradition, as if it was natural—something that had always been done. What was it about the social box that was so important?

My white boyfriend thought he was saving me from some sordid past. I lost my interest in the Flip gigs. I started hanging out with white kids, smoking pot, and dropping acid. I remember thinking—as though I'd chalked down decades of "worldly" life experience—that from about the age of ten to fifteen my life had been too wrapped up in the gigs and the Filipino community. I neglected my homework. I felt isolated from the rest of American life. When I reached the ripe old age of sixteen, I turned towards what seemed a wider and more sophisticated world, glad to put the dances behind me.

My mother continued to be heavily involved in the Filipino community. That world was an important social lifeline for her: my father's job took him far away, for months at a time, and she was lonely. Except for her daughter, all of her family members were overseas.

The social box and raffle ticket sales were finally replaced by other methods of raising money. The manongs were getting old and couldn't dance anymore. They suffered from arthritis and other debilitating health problems from doing stoop labor in the fields. They moved out of the labor camps and into their children's houses, or into low-cost apartments or elder care facilities. Filipinos arriving in the states during the late sixties, and later, were mostly professionals; some owned businesses and made hefty contributions to the Filipino community. There were still queen contests, but the winner was determined by her good grades, community service, talent and beauty. There were also debuts—they were "queenly" events too—and in some ways, just as competitive. But by that time, I had cut my ties from the Filipino community and tried my best to avoid their dances, banquets and get-togethers.

When I got older, I found my way back into the Filipino community through different routes—through writing, teaching, and researching Filipino American history. Now I have a lot of younger Filipina friends, who, it turns out, have in common with me the queen contest experience. It's a Filipina thing—we all know and laugh about it—sometimes grimly. At some point in our lives, many of us are publicly initiated into young womanhood by trial of queen contest or debut. And yet, my experience is not the same as theirs, and never will be. And I don't usually tell them about the social box, even though, when I look back, somehow it seemed like the centerpiece of all the Flip gigs. How do you explain something like that? "Well, it's sort of like taxi-dancing." But then you'd have to explain taxi-dancing—and it wasn't that. I think the social box marked the end of something, too—although I'm still not sure what that is...maybe a different way of being a Filipina within Filipino communities in the United States.

Several years ago, I thought to Google "social box" on the Internet.

There were many other Filipinas who had participated in the social box when I was young; certainly someone would write about it? But no, I couldn't find a thing.[3] Nothing, except for Norma Waterbury Thomas' missionary account of the social box. And I admit it made me feel a bit like an anomaly, or a ghost, as if I were the only Filipina in the world with that experience, and had only imagined it.

---

3. More recently, Dawn Bohulano Mabalon mentions the social box in *Filipinos in Stockton* (San Francisco: Arcadia, 2008), 95. I have found a few more brief references to the social box elsewhere, but there still appears to be very little detailed information available.

Discrimination and Struggle

LOVE LETTER FOR THE WOMEN OF THE WORLD
Kayla Crow

My life is the product of inspirational women. Women arrested for protesting the war, who occupied streets all around the world. Women who stand outside of hotels, fighting for workers' rights with bullhorns and leaflets, sometimes threatened or attacked. Women who work endlessly to make sure we have a choice, make sure we do not have to live silently in violent homes, and fight to ensure that one day, no matter where we live, we will be able to marry who we love.

These are the women who taught me how to speak in front of City Council, knock on strangers' doors, and channel myself to inspire and change my community.

My life is full of women who rise up, fight the wrongs in our world, women who have dedicated and sacrificed their lives, wholeheartedly, for the rest of us.

The first woman to inspire me was my *Lola*. After decades of raising and caring for 10 children, she came to the US, raised her grandchildren, and now helps raise the next generation. Her days have been spent working, cooking, cleaning, and making sure we all knew we were loved. That we always had family.

Her endless caring never left me, and will always remind me of the need for people who are willing to help others. People who are willing to care for the world. Maybe with a simple meal, a smile, and maybe a little TFC.

But this isn't simply about the women in my life.
This is for the women of the world.
Women fighting to survive everyday in war torn countries, occupied lands, women whose villages and towns no longer exist—
except within their eyes, their hands, their lips, their voice, their feet, and within the way their dreams will never let them forget the smell of home.

This is for the women who pursue an education, a job, a life, even when each goal and action is forbidden.

This is for the women who fight through every day, never knowing for certain that if they leave their homes, they'll make it back in one piece.

Kayla Crow

This is for the women who are seen as vessels, bodies, and not praised or worshipped as they should be—not just for creating future generation, but for molding and preparing them for the world.

This is for the women who risk everything: their lives, their families, their homes—
women who have been exiled, detained, tortured, and for the women who continue to fight long after.

Whether or not these women are here with us today, they have ignited the fire in all of us that will never be extinguished. A fire that will be passed down through the ages, hand in hand with our passion that moves mountains and inspires billions to rise, from India, to the U.S., to my family in Manila.

They are proof that being a woman has now become an act of revolution.

IN TRANSIT

Mel Vera Cruz

All things are in transit. Even in death all are "in the process" because decomposition is a kind of transit. Our body decays into another element for the benefit of all.

The *balikbayan* box symbolizes transit. Movement of stuff from one place to another so when we look into it, we'll find a variety of "unseen effects" that comes with it.

It is smuggling in the very sense of the word because we send this box full of goods outside this country without being taxed, but we let go of that because it stimulates the economy so no harm, no foul.

This box for me became a cultural symbol. The Filipino migrants' psyche can be compared to this and I think it should be noted.

It is made out of cardboard which is disposable, cheap, practical, and cheesy. A typical "third-world" label. This can cause any traveling *Pinoy* to feel uncomfortable when sat beside a person with Gucci luggage, but we don't bother because the *balikabayan* box is full of our selfless sacrifice and it don't matter anymore because we know it isn't important and it is not our priority.

We learn to block that insecurity because the people we care for are more important to us. All migrants know how hard it is to assimilate so that they can send stuff back home. So the *balikbayan* box for me means the opposite of cheap and cheesy. For me it represents strength, resilience and love, just like the main character of the Filipino psyche, and that's where I prefer to be.

The *balikbayan* box is *Pinoy* culture in transit. When you examine its contents, first things you'll see are Spam or maybe Vienna sausages. American products! We love it, but don't make an issue out of it because we've been owning everything since way back. Imagine *"tinikling"* was originally from India when I thought this was wholly ours. Damn! *Pansit* was Chinese, we have tons of Spanish words and we all love Elvis.

In return, immigrants are like imports. We bring our ways and attitudes wherever we go and that is the stimulus. We are the ones who stir America's culture. Everything that happens here can be traced from somewhere else. And it doesn't end here. Filipinos are spread all over the world so I'm pretty sure you'll be able to smell *adobo* anywhere you go.

Fusion is the word.

So I'd like to present my art just as it is, complete with "In your face" attitude, with warts and all because what matters is from within and this is a way for me to assert or transmit my energy that the common herd labeled "cheap."

These are some reasons why I work in this style with this material. They may be cheesy with some people who don't get it, but I have to present it with pride, confidence and attitude because I can see beneath it. I will not deny a part of me just because of what they think because I wouldn't be here if I took for granted some of the unique essence of my psyche. Just like any person from the "third-world," I have to be cockroach persistent for my message to be effective.

THE FIRST GRADE

BRENDA MANUEL FULTON

Mrs. Stanley was her name. Her skin was white as the clouds in the sky. She was a very tall woman with straight, beautiful light brown hair unlike my thick, wavy black hair. She spoke with a clear Alabama accent and her eyes were a cool blue. My teacher told us she came to California because her husband was in the military and stationed at Ford Ord in Monterey County. She was very pretty, but not really.

I never understood why Mrs. Stanley always gave me a look of hardness I had never known before. I'd bring her apples, save her a candy from my little brown bag of candies. I'd make her cards or I'd draw pretty pictures for her desk. I sat in the very front row, closest to her desk.

I could read really well, I had always done my schoolwork and was good, but that didn't help any when it came time for her to call on me for answers. I longed for my teacher to choose my hand up in the air so I could answer her questions correctly and she could see how smart I was, like all the white children she called to answer her many questions in our class. I waited for the day when she would finally call on me. I would answer correctly and then I'd get one of her big friendly smiles and so I sat with my arm up, sitting straight up, waiting and waiting for her to call on me. But I started noticing that she never gave me those big smiles she gave all the white children in my class and she never called on me.

Then the day finally came when she called my name. It wasn't what I had been waiting for anxiously each day at school. Mrs. Stanley scolded me. I remember her eyes looking like they'd come out of her head and her face reddened and her forehead became very wrinkled while she suddenly shouted at me to quit interrupting her and to be quiet. Her tone was very harsh. I hadn't interrupted her and I was so confused. Then she pointed for me to gather all my things out of the desk and move to the back of the row. I was so embarrassed and shocked, not knowing what I'd done wrong.

After this day she began to pick on me daily and ask me difficult questions. I knew she did not like me but could not figure out why. I would clam up and I could not get any words out of my mouth as she stood over me, repeating the question over and over. I could never get the words out correctly even though I knew the answer most of the time and I began stuttering. Mrs. Stanley began making fun of me, mimicking me and made all the children laugh at me. I began having difficulty speaking. I had to go to speech therapy at that time. In a home where my mother spoke with a heavy Mexican accent and my father spoke with a heavy Filipino accent, my words were pronounced sometimes with their confusing dialect at times.

I dreaded going to her class and felt badly about myself, not knowing what I had done so wrong or why she began treating me this way. I felt ashamed and scared to even look at her so I gave her no eye contact, stopped bringing her apples and candy and stopped drawing pictures for her desk. I lowered my head and I never raised my hand again or tried to answer any of her questions. I began to keep quietly to myself, never speaking because I was ashamed of my own voice. It was safer to remain quiet and in the back row. I began to do this in every class after I left the first grade.

Experiencing racism for the first time is difficult when one doesn't know what it is or why it exists. But when you are a person of color you learn to detect when someone doesn't like you for your color. It is in their eyes, body language and tone of voice and you will experience it over and over again in your lifetime and learn to recognize the ugliness of it.

WALLS AND A PLACE CALLED MANILA TOWN

Jeanette Gandionco Lazam

It is difficult to imagine the old International Hotel. It is difficult to imagine there were 56 good people who lived, worked, and loved there for so many years. It's also difficult to imagine, or to understand why 56 tenants stood firm on saving their home; stood righteous when the eviction notices were tacked on the doors of the Asian Community Center, the Chinese Progressive Association, Kearny Street Workshop, and last but not least, my home, the International Hotel.

Have you ever heard walls cry?

That's why the walls of the International Hotel had to be silenced, broken down, discarded and thrown away! The walls held the history and secrets of Filipinos.

As I stand here looking at this gaping hole of what used to be my home, my community, so many years have passed and so many of us have already passed on, into the light...into the "ever after."

Is there anyone left to tell our story? Is there anyone left to laugh at our jokes, taste our food, listen to our music and dance? I'm not sure, but I think it's just the ghosts who cling longingly to the walls in that gaping hole down below, wishing that someone, anyone please place their ear against the walls, then close their eyes and listen with their brothers, no matter how hot it got or how cold it was during the Alaskan Cannery season, they recognized the need to fight back and form unions.

They were never afraid... never!

It was too dangerous to allow the walls of the International Hotel to stay up right. It was too dangerous to allow the walls to creek and moan as they swayed with each punch from the wreaking ball. The walls screamed in such a high pitch only animals heard its mournful cry, the soulful weeping, the steady beating of the drum that sounded the alarm: THE EVICTION IS UPON US! THE EVICTION IS UPON US!

Someone said: THE WRITING IS ON THE WALL. What does that mean? Who wrote it and where did the writing go after the walls went down. I looked, and I only found eviction notices, death notices, late notices and little scraps of papers reminding us of those notices.

The writing on the wall, it was supposed to tell us that danger was imminent, that our time was running out...where should we go to save our walls... which way?

I looked for the mural wall. It told me to stand up and fight, to block the negative and punch with the positive. The mural sweated tears of blood for me; it cried every night someone placed a lit match too close to the open stove. But I turned away from the mural wall because it reminded me of what I was supposed to do: SAVE THE INTERNATIONAL HOTEL!

The hallway outside of my room, room 203 is dark, someone forgot to change the light blub. I don't care because I know how many footsteps it takes to reach the staircase, the toilet, and the end of the hallway where all our dreams have gone to die. I know because I hear the walls whispering those broken dreams of striking it rich and marrying a woman from the islands. 'THE ONLY THINGS THAT ARE TRULY BROKEN," says the whispering walls are the lives. Broken because the tenants believed too much and too late in the American dream.

Now, we are too old to remember what happened that night when they forced us to leave our home and our community. But I don't have to tell you that the walls remember it all.

During the Fall and Winter months, the walls gave us comforting heat; they shielded us from the rushing rainfall, the blustery wind that swept down Kearny Street. The walls guarded us from intruders who would otherwise strike the first blow to leave us homeless. But the walls grew tired and weary of all the tall tales, misguided love, hands lovingly touched by the grace of God, and silent stares of old men and women passing through the night.

In the Spring and Summer, we were held in by the glowing heat of the walls. We laid down on our beds, sweat and perspiration dripping from our bodies that made puddles of memories at the base of our feet. The walls grew hotter and hotter as each summer month descended upon us, choking the life out of us. The heat reminded us of the Philippines, a distant land that many had, so long ago, given up hope of ever returning. But walls would not let us forget.

The walls wailed in sorrow, in deep chords of aching pain as we, the tenants were removed one by one. They no longer were strong enough to keep the outsiders out, and the insider in. The hotel walls were just like the tenants, trying to hide so no one would hurt us. The walls, if they could only speak.

But they can, and they did the night of the eviction.

The walls of the International Hotel, *where have they gone?* They've gone to the sheet rock and plaster bins of history. *Why did they go there?* Because no one cared anymore for the stories it held. *When will they return?* Never, my friend. *How will we learn from them?* You'll learn from the tenants who remain to tell the story of the International Hotel. *Where shall I find them?* Wherever the fight for truth, justice and equality ring loud. In the hearts of those who march to a different drummer. Whose lives are the very walls that fought so hard and long to save not just a hotel, but a place called Manila Town.

CHALK DUST
Gwen Florelei Luib

I met Mrs. Sharon Smallwood during her first year teaching seventh grade history and religion at San Gabriel Academy, a small private Christian school I had attended since the first grade. On the first day of school, I saw her standing by her classroom door and greeting each student with a smile as we filed inside and found a vacant seat. She was a pretty African American woman, tall and slightly heavy-set. Her large brown eyes were the kind that bugged out from their sockets, dwarfing the other mouse-like features of her face, except her wide and gummy smile. I was struck most by the fact that she looked happy to see me, something that I rarely saw in the faces of the other teachers.

I was a horrible kid, often getting suspended from school for a variety of offenses, the main one being for fighting. When I was in the fourth grade, I was placed on in-school suspension for three days because I got into a fight with four other girls in my class. They started the fight, but I'm certain I had done something prior to that moment to have angered them. It happened during the first recess period of the day. I was walking by the playground monkey bars where the four of them sat like a wake of vultures, their faces in shadow as they stared down at me. I looked up at them and they jumped me. Four-to-one. They out-numbered me, but I didn't care. As the girls and the dust of the playground yard started to swirl around me, I felt possessed as I pulled hair, scratched faces, punched stomachs, and kicked shins.

I developed a taste for fighting that day, threatening to beat up other kids and teachers when they would do something I believed was unfair or hurtful to me. I felt like my fists were the only way I could make myself heard, the only way I could get some kind of justice whenever I perceived that I had been wronged. I was looking for a way to let out a rage that was born out of an experience from early infancy—a story about an abusive babysitter that my parents would not tell me until many years later. But that is a different story.

For all the years I caused problems at San Gabriel Academy, I was never kicked out. Perhaps it was because it was a Christian school and the administration believed in practicing forgiveness. I'm not really sure. Most likely, I think it was because my parents paid for me to be there. All I know was that no amount of money could change the fact that I was troubled, misunderstood, and unable to make any real connections with other people. I say this, now years later, with a certain amount of emotional distance. But the truth is that I was miserably lonely.

During the recess breaks, I watched with envy as the other kids in my class sat together under a line of trees in the schoolyard, their legs crossed Indian-style on the grass, chattering about things that made them smile. I was ashamed to see myself reflected in their eyes and frowns whenever I tried to join them. And when the school bell rang, I was shamed even more to see the annoyance in the cold eyes and strained smiles of my other teachers when I walked into their classrooms. I knew they all hated me, and I carried that knowledge with me everywhere until I hated myself too. And every day I grew more and more depressed and angry by the thought that there was nothing I could do to change things.

I sat in the front row of Mrs. Smallwood's class. I always liked sitting in front, feeling that it was the best place to be when a teacher would ask a question. There, I could easily be seen, could easily let the teacher know that I knew the answer as I raced to raise my hand first and wave it in the air.

While other teachers would call on the first student with his or her hand up, which I always tried to make sure was me, Mrs. Smallwood was different. She would ignore me and call on other students who could never seem to know the right answer. After a couple of days of being ignored, I started to snap my fingers as I raised my hand, thinking that it would help her better notice me.

My snapping fingers didn't go over well with Mrs. Smallwood. One day she asked me to stay after class, and once we were alone, she looked me in the eye and told me that she didn't appreciate being snapped at. She spoke in a low voice, almost whispering, as if she wanted to keep me from the embarrassment of anyone else hearing that I was being scolded. She said that she knew I had the answers to her questions, but she wanted to give the other kids a chance to show they knew the answers too. Then she warned me, saying that if I didn't learn to control myself, she'd keep me after school to clean the blackboards which were usually clouded with the stain of yellow or white chalk by the end of the day.

I knew Mrs. Smallwood meant what she was saying but change is hard. The very next day, I was snapping my fingers at her again and was given a weeklong detail of chalkboard-cleaning every day after school. Every afternoon I had to wipe the boards with the chalkboard erasers. Then I was given a bucket to bring to the bathroom and fill with heavy water, which I then had to lug back to the classroom. I would dunk a clean rag into the warm water, twist it up and wring it out, before running it along the blackboard. With every rub and wipe, I watched the white or yellow fog of chalk disappear section by section until the board's black color could finally be seen. And when that was done, I went outside and clapped the chalkboard erasers together and watch the cloudbursts of chalk dust rise up and into the air.

After a week of cleaning the blackboards, the punishment for my bad behavior became something else more significant. As I wiped the remnants of lessons off the boards, Mrs. Smallwood would talk to me and ask me questions. We would discuss the daily history and religion lessons and the value of revolution and change. She asked me what my hobbies were and what I liked to do. I enjoyed talking to her so much that even after I had stopped snapping my fingers and my afterschool detention had ended, I volunteered to stay after school to wash the boards, saying that I wanted to do it.

I had been cleaning her chalkboards for almost a month when Mrs. Smallwood asked me a surprising question. Her preamble to the question was a sequence of casual statements spoken in a way that seemed like she was merely musing aloud.

"You know, I was warned about you," she said. "During my teaching orientation this summer, they called you 'The Devil's Child.'"

I was in the middle of rubbing a particularly dirty section of the board when she said this. My hand dropped and I froze. I stared at the chalkboard still waiting to be cleaned. I was afraid of what she was going to say next, afraid to turn around and see that she was staring at me coldly or with a frown on her face.

"But, I think they're wrong," I heard her say. She paused before she continued. "I think you're sweet and that you only act the way you do because you don't think anyone hears you. Do you think they were wrong?"

I didn't answer. I couldn't because I wanted to cry. I wasn't surprised to discover my nickname, which simply stated what I felt was the truth of who I was. What shocked me was that Mrs. Smallwood was saying they were wrong, that I was wrong to have agreed with them. And if I was wrong about that, there was a chance I was wrong about everything else.

Sensing Mrs. Smallwood's eyes on my back as she waited for an answer, I glanced at her and saw the warmth still there in her eyes and smile. I nodded and grinned back at her. Before she could ask me anything else, I grabbed the chalkboard erasers, walked outside, and clapped them together, hard like the rest of my life depended on it. And as the dust clouds of chalk gathered

Gwen Florelei Luib

around me and mixed with my tears, I could feel the weight of the shame and loneliness and hopelessness I carried rise slowly up and out of me, until I was watching them float higher and higher into the sky.

THE TWO USAS
OSCAR PEÑARANDA

I don't know about you but more and more lately I've been seeing two USAs. There is the USA of the white people and the USA of the people of color. There are two USAs. There is the USA of the men and the USA of the women. There are two USAs. There is the USA of the rich and the upper middle class who are trying to be rich and the USA of the poor and the working-class people. There are two USAs. There is the USA of the heterosexuals and the USA of the homosexuals. There are two USAs. There is the USA of the Judeo-Christians and the USA of the non-Judeo Christians. There are two USAs; there is the USA of the "able" and the USA of the "dis-abled," even though the "disabled" are more able than some of the "ables."

Which one are you? Where are you at? Which ones do you see?

Do you belong to the ones who want to dismantle the schism or do you belong to the ones who don't care and by not caring and doing, keep the USA divided?

There are two USAs. There is the USA of monoculturalism and the USA of multiculturalism. If it is not plural it is singular. For there are two USAs. There is the USA who says *E pluribus Unum* and the USA who does *E Pluribus Unum*. There is the USA who says the constitution and the USA who lives and does the constitution.

There is the USA who would rather keep silent about racism the better to pretend that it does not exist anymore or that it might go away if left untouched or that things are much better now. And the USA who wants to have it out, dialogue, take actions, and dismantle the racism. And that not everything is better, and that some things are better but some things are just as bad, and some things even worse.

There are two USAs. There is the USA who calls the USA America, and the USA who calls the USA, USA. Or Amerika with a "k," or "U.S. American." For the latter, America is a hemisphere, half the world, not just one country, a most inexact misnomer, not just geographically. For the former, and many, if not all, our leaders in politics (including presidents), and all our media of television newscasters and announcers of any event, films, all our schools including commissions of standardized tests, and as a result, an overwhelming majority of citizens, to them the place USA is synonymous with the place America. Ask the other non-Americans who live in America if they feel slighted, insulted, and bereft of their dignity and identities, when another country call their homeland's name as only that country's own.

Now this I don't have to remind or point out to you. There are two USAs. There is the USA of television and movies. Then there is the USA of reality and everyday living. California is now 56% people of color, and the whites a minority and continuously being surpassed in numbers all throughout the country. Yet everything reflected about California, in the movies, in T.V. programs are all overwhelmingly white. Sometimes exclusively white. That is not the real California, as what is being portrayed all throughout our T.V. and movie screen are not the real USA.

There are two USAs. There is the USA of the textbooks and the curriculum and the USA that is not in the textbooks and the curriculum, even though in many cases their student population make up the majority of the people in the classrooms who read and study those books. Where do you stand here?

There are two USAs, one with a heritage of one language and one with the heritage of more than one language. Where are you here?

There are two USAs, one who sees only one USA or the one who sees the two. Which one are you now?

First published in *Poor Magazine* (http://poormagazine.org)

A QUESTIONABLE LEGACY

Victoria Santos

1939

Six months after Mom and Dad eloped, police went through their apartment in Muncie, Indiana looking for stolen property. Dad had been working for two photographers—two sisters—who had a downtown studio. He did retouching and helped out in the darkroom, developing and printing pictures. Mom said that during one week, students came in to have their high school graduation pictures taken. They wandered in and out of the reception rooms as they waited their turns.

"One evening," Mom said, "two officers knocked on our apartment door. The two sisters had filed a complaint against Dad. They said he had taken some rings that had gone missing."

"Over our objections," she continued, "the police searched our place and found nothing because Dad was innocent of the charges. We knew it was because we were Filipinos."

My mother rarely spoke about being discriminated against, but when I asked her once about it, she recalled this instance so clearly, as if it had just happened.

When I was five or six, we lived in a predominantly black neighborhood on the near northside of Chicago. It was after World War II. People couldn't distinguish Filipinos from Japanese then and my brother and I were often subjected to anti-Japanese epithets when we walked to school.

One day, I went alone to play with my friend, Margie, on the next block. Hers was the only other Filipino family in the area. Her brother was the same age as mine and we were often at each other's home.

When I left her place, I was cornered by three older black girls who taunted me with words like "you little Jap girl." Before I knew it, I was in a hallway and they were taking turns beating me up. When they finally let me go, I ran home. Mom and Dad comforted me, but I was never allowed to go over to Margie's again. It was so long ago I don't remember the physical pain, but the memory of it lingers.

1996

Nuno and I spent a night in San Francisco when our son was seven years old. A close friend had volunteered to keep him so we could have dinner alone and take in a play, something we rarely did since he came into our lives. Like a lot of couples we knew who had wanted a child for a long time, we had a hard time separating from him, choosing activities in which we could include him. It wasn't until my friend pointed out that we were turning into boring parents and needed to take time to ourselves that we planned this date. We splurged and reserved a room off Union Square, close to the restaurant and theater.

After checking into our hotel, we walked out into the cool evening air on Geary Boulevard before turning up Powell. Nuno looked particularly handsome in his navy blazer, tailored slacks, and tie. I wore a midnight blue dress with a necklace Nuno had bought for me when we were in Juneau. We so rarely dressed up but this was a special evening.

We took care to cross Powell carefully so my heels wouldn't get caught in the cables. It was just a short three or four blocks to the theater. I remember how light and carefree we felt, happy in our twosomeness.

As we made our way uphill, a middle-aged man veered into our path. He was unshaven, his drab green and black camouflage jacket and pants wrinkled, and he was in need of a bath. His scowl and narrow eyes focused on me as he neared. I braced myself for I-don't-know-what but I suspected it wasn't good. Nuno was oblivious to the impending danger I sensed in this man. Out of nowhere, the man let loose a stream of venom directed at me.

"Go back to where you come from, you fuckin' Asian bitch!" And he continued mumbling profanities under his breath.

Nuno's inclination was to step around the malcontent and keep walking.

Not me. I was enraged at this stranger verbally accosting me in this fashion for no other reason than that I was Asian.

From deep within me came the words, "Shut the hell up. Don't you speak to me in that way. I was born and raised here like a lot of people who look like me. And you can go to hell!"

Nuno was aghast at my retort, but he knew not to interrupt me. He told the vagrant to get away from us and I think the man was so startled by my response, he shrunk back in silence.

I was fuming but energized by the exchange. It was one of those rare moments when my mouth was in sync with my brain and my emotions.

It was probably foolish of me, but I felt like the guy in that movie, "I'm mad as hell and I'm not going to take it anymore."

2009

After a dinner party at our house, we asked our then 20-year-old son to drive a guest home to San Jose. It was after midnight. After more than two hours, we became worried because it had started raining heavily and the drive shouldn't have taken more than an hour.

When Thomas returned, he was visibly upset.

"We got pulled over by the police. They searched the car and patted us down." He was pacing back and forth, his clothes drenched, hair dripping.

"What happened?" I asked.

"We were on Santa Clara Avenue when I came to a red light. I couldn't see the pedestrian crosswalk lines and I came to a stop just over the lines.

I saw two police cars parked at the intersection. As soon as I got through the intersection, they pulled me over."

Thomas' passenger was a young engineering intern who had just arrived from Portugal the day before and was going to work in Nuno's office for a few months as part of an exchange program. We could only imagine what was going through his mind.

"I gave the officer my license and proof of insurance. He asked if I had been drinking. I said I had had a sip of your port wine. Then he asked if he was going to find any drugs if he searched the car. I told him I didn't do drugs."

My son had been wearing a polo shirt and slacks, had just had his hair trimmed, so he was looking pretty clean cut, as was Fernando, the intern.

"The officer asked us to get out of the car and patted us down, then another went through the glove compartment and trunk."

"They didn't find anything," he said, "then they let us get back in the car. The officer just said there were a number of people involved in drug dealing on that street and we should be careful."

I could see my son standing against the car in the pouring rain, being subjected to this indignity and I was angry. Two young men in a car after midnight, stopped and frisked, all for driving while brown.

When I hear of racial profiling in the news, I can't avoid thinking of how racism and discrimination have affected my own family over three generations, over more than seven decades, and how little has changed since that day in 1939, in Muncie, Indiana, when the police knocked on my parents' door.

A couple of non-Asian, non-Filipino friends will tell me they never think of me as Asian or Filipino. I know they mean that as a compliment and I know that is their intent, but I still have mixed feelings about that. Because fitting in as "just another American" has never come easily and I think people of color never take that for granted. Because just when I think we've made progress as a diverse nation, especially after electing an African-American to the White House, one little incident can make me think that in 2014, we still have a long way to go.

HUMAN REMOVAL

Juanita Tamayo Lott

I cannot even show you
The house I first lived in
When I came to this place
When I was two years old

It was the first floor of an ugly-blue-gray-two-story-flat
On Laguna Street between Bush and Sutter
It was in that marginal neighborhood
Which demarcates the poor blacks of the Fillmore from the
Powerful whites of Pacific Heights

We lived—my mother, my father, my sister, and I
We lived in a one bedroom flat
We lived in the living room
Two elderly Pilipino men, relatives of my mother lived in the bedroom
And all of us shared the kitchen and bathroom

I remember some good moments in that old kitchen
With bare bulbs hanging from a high ceiling
When friends came for dinner and everyone talked and laughed
But I also remember my mother weeping silently
Over the kitchen sink
Tears falling down her cheek and onto
Her big belly carrying my brother
And I knew even at four that she wished we had our own flat

Juanita Tamayo Lott

My mother's wish came true
And the old flat remained for a few more years
To house someone else's tears and smiles

And one day, not too long ago
When I was walking along the demarcation line,
I stopped and turned on Laguna Street to visit that old flat
But it was no longer there

In its place was a vacant lot and a sign about urban renewal

First published in *Summary and Recommendations: Conference on Pacific/Asian American Families and HEW Related Issues* by the U.S. Department of Health, Education and Welfare, May, 1978

EDUCATING JUSTINE

Justine Villanueva

My mother keeps mementos: my dried umbilical cord, my white leather christening shoes, the program from my kindergarten graduation program, news articles about my tennis matches, my medals and trophies. She keeps things that I have long ago discarded but she deems important.

Several months ago, I visited her in her Daly City home. "I've been keeping these," she told me. She handed me three documents in plastic sheet protectors: a copy of my birth certificate, my U.S. citizenship certificate, and, something that I had never shown her before, my acceptance letter from UC Berkeley.

"*Nadawat diay ka sa UC Berkeley?*" she asked, her voice barely audible.

I sensed tension. "Yep," I teased, "back when I was still smart, Mom, before I turned *bugok* from all these years of living in America!" I walked away to the kitchen. I did not want her to ask any more because I did not know how to answer her without sounding arrogant and foolish and sad and right and wrong all at the same time.

I thought of the day that letter arrived, twenty years ago. "Letter for you from UC Berkeley," the postman said as he handed me the envelope. He had a thick Chinese accent that was hard to understand. "My daughter got in. The envelope looked just like this! Good luck to you!"

My heart raced and my fingers trembled when I ripped open the envelope. When I read the word "Congratulations," I screamed my joy and did the running man move all over our living room. No one was home to hear or see me. My mother worked as a stay-in nursing aide at a retirement home during the week and only came home during the weekend. My two older brothers also worked as personal assistants to several elderly patients and they rarely had days off.

"*Nganong wala man ka nagsulti?*" My mom followed me to the kitchen. I did not know how long she had been keeping that letter, waiting for the right moment to ask me this question. She needed an answer. "*Sayang kaayo,*" she sighed. My chest tightened and I pursed my lips to prevent angry words from spewing out. I consoled myself that at least she did not say, "*Sayang ka kaayo*" which would have meant that I was such a waste.

I had heard this word before, *Sayang*, almost in the same context. A few months before my parents made the arrangements to have us reunite with them in America, I had graduated from my high school and been accepted to UP Diliman. My aunt in Manila, who strongly believed in getting a university education, had taken it upon herself to plan my transition from living in Malaybalay, a small town in the Southern Philippines, to Manila. When she found out I was going to leave for America, instead of attending the highest rated university in the whole country, my aunt made the trip to my grandfather who was taking care of me while my parents were away, and lamented, "*Sayang! Sayang!*" They placed a long distance phone call to my mother and begged her, "Let Justine stay with me, Julie. Let her get a college degree first. She doesn't have to go to America, especially not right away. Very few get accepted to UP, you know that. What is she going to do when she gets there, at her age? *Sayang kaayo*, Jul!"

No amount of begging, admonishing, and cursing worked. After years of living apart, my mother wanted the family to be together the soonest time possible. There was no argument against that, not even the promise of a really good college education.

When I arrived in the U.S., I was sixteen, still too young to attend the local city college and too young to start working full time as a nurse aide or a nanny, a personal assistant, or any of the other jobs my family had. So instead of attending UP Diliman, I attended El Camino High School. I fit in without too much problem: I spoke English with hardly any accent because of all my years of learning English as a second language; I took Physics and Calculus; I sang in musical productions; I romped in the catacombs and took photos next to tombstones; I wore bell bottoms purchased from thrift shops; I dated an "American" boy with fine blond hair and we went to the senior prom together. High school was my introduction to America. Except for the few fights over boyfriends and girlfriends, high school for me was a fairly safe place. In high school, it didn't matter whether I was a "resident."

I did not know what "residency" meant. I thought my residency started when I arrived and started residing in California. When I started to apply for college and had to fill out application papers, I claimed to be a California resident. By the time acceptance letters were mailed out, I had realized that my claimed residency needed to be evidenced by a green card. That was a problem because I did not have a green card. Then I realized something even more problematic: I did not have any legal status. My father had left his petitioner employer prior to my arrival in America and he never got his H employment status converted to a green card. When his H visa expired, he became a *TnT*. His dependents, my mother and my siblings, also became *TnT*.

I started feeling the burden of this realization. I felt it when my grandfather passed away in the Philippines and my father, already out of status, could not attend the funeral. I felt it when my mother and brothers complained about how their employers mistreated them and yet they did not dare leave because jobs were hard to find and, more importantly, they did not want to be reported to Immigration. I felt it when my aunt paid someone thousands of dollars to marry her and petition for her green card. I felt it when my uncle stopped going to the tennis courts because he did not know how to answer when other Filipinos would casually ask whether he was already a citizen or still a green card holder.

I also started to worry about being at UC Berkeley, needing to show proof of residency and having nothing. I worried even more that my non-residency meant that for tuition purposes, we would have to pay thousands and thousands of dollars. How were my parents ever going to afford to send me to UC Berkeley?

The noise of water spraying out of the faucet filled the kitchen. I relaxed my jaw and took a deep breath. "Mom," I said, focusing on her gray hair, "if you really want to know why I never told you about being accepted at UC Berkeley, it was because we were *TnT*. I was scared and embarrassed to be one. The school was asking me for all sorts of papers to show residency and we didn't have any to show." I shrugged even though she could not see me do it. "But also, being a non-resident meant that even if it was okay for me to attend the university as a non-resident, it would have been very, very expensive to send me there. I didn't think you could have afforded it and I didn't want you to feel bad or guilty about it. So I didn't tell you." I did not add that I resented her for this for a long time. I shrugged again. "But that's all in the past. I probably would not have survived there, anyway. That place is big! It's probably as big as Malaybalay, with as many people! And it's far from Daly City. I'll take you there for a visit, if you want, so you can see."

My mother continued to rinse the plates. Finally, without turning around to look at me, she sighed, "Still, you should have told me. I could have done it, you know." She sounded sad and proud. "I sacrificed everything I had to come here to America so that I could give you a good life. I worked hard all those years for a reason. I don't know why you didn't think I could have done it. I would have done it if you had let me." I felt my chest tighten again and I had to purse my lips to stop my tears from falling. "*Sayang*" she repeated, the gush of the faucet almost drowning her soft voice.

I still keep that acceptance letter from UC Berkeley in my safe along with my U.S. passport and citizenship certificate.

BEEF STEW, MAYBE TRIPE

Peter Kenichi Yamamoto

I cry tears of loss and pain for you, Al
My tears always fall from tight-clenched eyes like a light spring rain in a lush forest jungle.
Prelude to a Spring monsoon torrent rain in the Pacific and South Asia.
It hurts so much inside.

Al, I can't believe that we have lost you.
Never again to rap with you, talk story,
Or break bread with you. The crispy
skin of the *lechon*.

To hear you say: "It's gonna be all right!"
Or: "Love you, Brother!" and hug you, when we parted.
To see your high forehead and glasses above a grey mustache and beard.
Your straight body, unbent, unbroken.

You seemed a young 68 years,
Though you were really 79.
How many friendships.
How many connections with us, of yours.

We are mourning you, Al.
We are grieving.
Manong Tony says you are STILL in the hospital.
The counter girl at Happy Donuts already told him that you had passed.

Peter Kenichi Yamamoto

You are now rapping with the *Manongs* of the I-Hotel. With
Manong Felix Ayson and Manong Claudio Domingo. Sorria
is with you with his cooking pots. Agnes and Manong
Wahat Tompao too.

Is Joe Diones coming after you waving his pistol? And
Sammy the Flower Man with his stolen blossoms? And
Manong Freddy with his banjo? You are there with them
again now, Al.

You are there with them laughing at us.
Or with us.
Gently asking if we have had our breakfast yet
Remembering the stained counters and lazy flies of Silverwing Cafe and Star Lunch

You are there with the Pinoys of Lucky M Pool Hall.
Lounging in dark corners.
Hovering over green felt pool tables
With slender cues in their gnarled hands under felt hats and naked lightbulbs.

You are there watching the Manongs line up
To be seen by the young Pinay nurse
At Manilatown.
We talked about the fine young Sisters in our lives too.

You, me, Lou Syquia and Lamonta,
At Manilatown
Talking about my stacks of hard bound Journals
Talking about the fine young sisters in our lives.

Peter Kenichi Yamamoto

I remember the old I-Hotel.
Me, an itinerant young man college dropout worker. The low
faded green wood bench in front of the I-Hotel A bag of *char
siu bao* in my hand, thoughtfully munching.

You pass by on your way to the original old Kearny Street Workshop
To see...what were their names? Names?

Jim Dong. Nancy Horn. Leland Wong. Presco Tabios. Norman Jayo. Jimmy Yee. Richard Likong. Doug Yamamoto. Crystal Huie. Dennis Taniguchi. Lou Syquia. Judy Talogan. George Leong. Dean Tom. Nelson Yee. Sachiko Nakamura, Brenda Aoki. Genny Lim. Russell Leong. Geraldine Kudaka. Bob Hsiang. And so many more...

You remember the Manongs to the youth.
To the barrio kids in the South of Market schools and youth groups.
Telling the stories of salmon fish head soup and
Stockton taxi-dances, with pomade hair, Florsheim shoes, and Blondies.

My Chinese immigrant restauranteur friend says:
"Your friend in heaven looking down at you now,
He want you look happy!" Yes Al, you want me
look happy?

Sadnesses falling away to emptinesses and lonelinesses.
Without you anymore Al.
Like when we lost Brother Bill Sorro too.
What we gonna do now, Al?

Who's gonna round up the old-timers?
And who's gonna get together the poets?

Peter Kenichi Yamamoto

And who's gonna make the festivals a happening place?
Who's gonna point out those fine points of humanity and struggle?

The old Pinoy in the wheelchair living in the Mission District. He
doesn't know you are gone. The Nisei homeless old lady living
on Clement Street. She doesn't know you're gone.

Who's gonna tell all your elderly friends locked up in their lonely hotel rooms?
Who's gonna publish all your stories of the Manong that you hold in your mind?
You're gone away. Like a whispy trailing wind.

We already miss you too much.
And already you are forgotten because you aren't here to speak for yourself.
BUT I DON'T FORGET YOU!!!!
Like I don't forget the Brother Bill Sorro!!!

Do you remember the three of us at Tule Lake Pilgrimage.
Bill Sorro, me, and you?
Three crazy m.f.'ers in the back of the bus!
Stone crazy artists and lovers and Third World revolutionaries.

Al Robles came out of the old International Hotel struggle,
With others on the Mayor's committee you fought
For the New I-Hotel.
Some bricks from the old I-Hotel are in the New I-Hotel's Manilatown Center.

The fight of those Manongs and the elderly Chinese is over.
And the New I-Hotel stands tall, imposing, and proud at Kearny and Jackson Streets.
A monument to their long painful community struggle.
Section 8 Senior Low-income Housing.

Peter Kenichi Yamamoto

Al Robles is gone
But he lives on in the search of the young ones coming up.
Who see the New I-Hotel arisen.
And who hear the story of the *Manong*.

Laborers in the canneries of Alaska.
The strawberry and lettuce fields of Salinas.
The apple and pear orchards of Sacramento.
The hotels of San Francisco.

You loved your food, your cafeteria-style "buffets"
Your down-home neighborhood eateries and "dives"
Food was forever big with you.
As it was to be with a beautiful woman.

Al, I miss your Zen-like rapping.
Out there yet controlled.
With a method to your madness.
Wisdom in a few words and observances.

And always that warmth.
That warmth.
That love that is so typical of you, Al.
It's a stereotype to say it.

But that love of the people.
The young and the old.
The good and the not-so-good.
Like a beef-stew of life. Maybe tripe.

Peter Kenichi Yamamoto

Or spaghetti with eggs over easy at Pork Chop House.
On a quiet, foggy San Francisco morning.
Give way to the brave wan sunshine of a new Spring day.
...And you, Al.

Myrna Ziálcita • Evangeline Canonizado Buell
Edwin Lozada • Eleanor Hipol Luis • Evelyn Luluquisen • Tony Robles

Photograph: Courtesy of Joshua Isaacs
www.jjisaacs.com
https://www.facebook.com/joshisaacsphotography

Biographies

JEFFREY TANGONAN ACIDO
...was born in Ilocos Norte and grew up in Kalihi, Kawaii. He is a PhD candidate in Education at the University of Hawaii at Manoa. He hopes to build a center for popular education and ancestral wisdom where people can learn and heal with each other.

JEANNIE BARROGA
...Dramatists Guild member —plays: *Buffalo'ed*, W.A. Gerbode/Hewlett Foundation Collaboration with Alleluia Panis; *Walls*, NEA Artistic Excellence grant; and *Banyan*, 2009 Arty Award for Best Original Production (11 of 37 nominations). National productions: *Walls*; *Eye of the Coconut*; *Talk-Story* and more. Direction: *Korean Badass*, LaMama's, NY and AARRS recovery program, Brava Theater Center. Ms. Barroga was AATC's Interim Artistic Director and TheatreWorks' first literary manager. Current projects: *Marked*, mystery paranormal novel; *I Am a Ghost*, *Crazed*, *First Morn*, *Prophecy of Eve* (actor).
Website: www.jeanniebarroga.com   Twitter @jeanniebarroga

RENELAINE BONTOL-PFISTER
...Her flash fiction, "Crab", was published in Vintage Voices 2012 by the Redwood Writers in Sonoma County, California. Sonoma watercolor artist, Sally Baker, chose her short story "Cherries for Bidu" to accompany one of her paintings. She wrote a column in New Jersey from 2006-2008, and her short stories, poems and essays have been published in the Philippines.

TITANIA BUCHHOLDT
...is a lifetime member of the Alaska chapter of the Filipino American National Historical Society. Kindly visit her mother's memorial website at www.ThelmaBuchholdt.com.

EVANGELINE CANONIZADO BUELL
...author, writer, activist, recipient of community awards, folk singer guitarist, mother, grandmother and great grandmother, and wife to Bill, the other half of her heart. Her parents were born in the Philippines and came to the U.S. in the 1920s. Vangie was born in California, raised in the Bay Area, and lived all of her adult life in the city of Berkeley. Her professional goals have focused on promoting cultural understanding on both the local and international levels. She served as Public Events manager of the International House at UC Berkeley and Program Coordinator of the Consumers Cooperative of Berkeley, Inc. She taught folk guitar, performed on concert stage, radio and TV and is the recipient of several awards for community activism, the FANHS Silver Arts and Music Award, and the 100 Most Influencial Filipina Women in the U.S. award from the Filipina Women's Network. Vangie has three daughters, Danni, Nikki, and Stacey Vilas; two granddaughters, Quiana and Brielle; a grandson, Joshua; and a great grandson Zachary Jordan Isaacs.

TESS CRESCINI
...was born in Pasay City and immigrated to the U.S. at age 14 with her father. She recently graduated with a Masters of Arts in Engaged Humanities and the Creative Life with emphasis in Depth Psychology at Pacifica Graduate Institute. She is currently working on short story cycles compiled for a book about a young Filipina immigrant coming to terms with her authentic Self.

KAYLA CROW
...is a writer and community organizer in Long Beach, CA where she has lived for 20 years. Along with writing for websites like www.musicinpresss.com, she has been writing poetry inspired and dedicated to the work of Anakbayan Los Angeles, of which she is a member. She lives by the Mahmoud Darwish idea that "every beautiful poem is an art of resistance."

MEL VERA CRUZ
...is an artist living in the East Bay Area who migrated from the Philippines when he was 31. He's been an artist since 5 years of age. He has been showing his works in Manila, Philippines, and parts of the U.S., particularly in Oakland and San Fran-

cisco, CA. He had 9 years in an advertising agency as illustrator and art director and presently works as a digital printer and tattoo artist.

ANN FAJILAN
... is an Associate Theatre Professor at California State University, East Bay. In addition to teaching theater core classes, she also teaches Applied Theatre Tactics for Social Justice, Creative Direction & Communities and Dramatic Activities for children. She is currently developing The Legacy Project which dramatizes the oral histories of California Filipinos from the Bridge Generation through the Sixties. She is simultaneously adapting Vangie Buell's *25 Chickens and a Pig for a Bride* into a loving folk musical.

BRENDA MANUEL FULTON
...is half Filipino-American and half Mexican-American. She always felt confused about where she belonged until she first joined the Berkeley writing group at the time headed by the wonderful writer and editor, Helen Toribio. When Brenda began sharing and writing her stories about our backyard excitement of pig preparations for weddings, chicken fights, social box dances and other stories, she realized she was more Filipino than she thought, "...other than my flat nose." She is an artist, writer and mother living in Northern California.

WILFRED GALILA
...Born and raised in the Philippines, Wilfred Galila is in the pursuit of deciphering the ramifications of cultural hybridity in his postcolonial mind. He currently lives in the San Francisco Bay Area.

MICHELE GUTIERREZ
...is a second-generation Filipina, born and raised in Long Beach, CA. A graduate of UCLA, an Armed With a Camera Fellow and a Voice of Our Nations (VONA) alum, she is a writer, teacher and community activist. Her writing can be found in *Field of Mirrors: An Anthology of Philippine American Writers* (2008), *Maganda Magazine*, *Our Own Voice*, and other venues. She is currently writing a memoir entitled "The Spaces We Fill."

Herb Jamero
...is a second generation Filipino American and has written stories and poems mainly about his heritage that have been featured in the *Filipino Journal* and other publications. He is a retired Psychiatric Social Worker specializing in youth and families. He now resides in Livingston, CA on the family ranch—the original site of the Jamero Farm Labor Camp which housed up to 100 Filipino farm laborers. He is the Historian of the FANHS-Central Valley Chapter.

Jessica Jamero
...is a Central Valley native and graduate of California State University, Fresno. She currently teaches high school English.

Emily Porcincula Lawsin
...is originally from "SHE-attle," Washington, is a Trustee of the Filipino American National Historical Society, co-founder of the Detroit Asian Youth Project, and co-author of *Filipino Women in Detroit*. She has taught Asian American Studies at UCLA, California State University, Northridge, and University of Michigan. An oral historian and spoken word performance poet since 1990, she has appeared on radio and stage throughout the U.S. and Manila.

Jeanette Gandionco Lazam
was born and raised in New York City's Lower East Side; as such her soul belongs to Manhattan, but her heart belongs in Hawai'i and the Philippines...divided respectfully!" She currently resides in Berkeley, CA with 5 cats, 2 killer parakeets, and her housemate, Annie.

Juanita Tamayo Lott
...has written for both scholarly and public audiences since 1968 from poetry to statistical analyses. Her creative writing is in *Liwanag, Asian Women, Third World Women,* and *The American Poetry Review*. She has read her poems on KPFA-FM Berkeley, CA, WPFW-FM Washington, DC, San Francisco State University, the Library of Congress and the Smithsonian Institution, among other venues.

Edwin Agustín Lozada

...teaches Spanish language and literature at Woodside High School and is the Co-Chair of its World Languages Department. He has two books of poetry from Carayan Press, *Sueños anónimos/Anonymous Dreams* (2001), *Bosquejos/Sketches* (2003) and is the editor of two PAWA anthologies, *Field of Mirrors: An Anthology of Philippine American Writers* (2008), *Remembering Rizal, Voices from the Diaspora* (2011). He is a board member of Philippine American Writers and Artists, Inc. (PAWA).

Gwen Florelei Luib

...is a Filipina-Canadian writer and educator who was born in Manila but raised in Toronto and Los Angeles. A graduate of the MFA in Creative Writing program at San Jose State University and an alumna of the 2012 and 2013 Voices of Our Nations (VONA) Writing Workshop, she has received several awards for her poetry, fiction, and screenwriting. When she is not writing or teaching, she helps run an open mic called Sunday Jump in Historic Filipinotown in Los Angeles and assists in library-building projects in both of her parents' hometowns in the Philippines.

Eleanor (Ellie) Hipol Luis

...a first generation Filipina, was born and raised in the East Bay to parents from San Fernando, La Union (Ilocano) and San Antonio, Basey (Visayan). She has worked four-plus decades in the College of Ethnic Studies at San Francisco State University and is co-author of *Images of America: Filipinos in the East Bay* and published in *Seven Card Stud with Seven Manangs Wild*. Ellie is married to musician Ben Luis and has three sons, Joachim, Paulo and Valentino and a daughter-in-law, Ligaya. Her family continues to grow together through their life experiences and especially with the addition of three grandchildren: Maksim Atlee, Jordyn Stella and Kaiyen Eve.

Evelyn Luluquisen

...was born in Oakland, California. She spoke Ilocano before learning English in school. She received a bachelors degree in Environmental Studies from the University of California, Santa Cruz. She was appointed Executive Director for the Manilatown Heritage Foundation in 2010 and is co-author of *Filipinos in the East Bay* and project lead for *Filipinos in San Francisco*, books published by Arcadia Publishing Company. She is active in the Filipino American National Historical Society as a book editor, oral history interviewer, proposal writer, and history advocate. Evelyn dabbles in the performing arts as an actor and playwright; is a volunteer history docent for the Oakland Museum of California, and worked in the field of human resources for the University of California, Berkeley.

Rebecca Mabanglo-Mayor

...is the pen name of Rebecca Saxton. She received her MFA in Creative Writing from Pacific Lutheran University in 2012. Her poetry and short fiction have appeared in *Katipunan Literary Magazine* and the online magazine *Haruah*. Her short story "Yellow is for Luck" appears in the anthology *Growing Up Filipino II: More Stories for Young Adults*, edited by Cecilia Brainard. Her poetry chapbook *Pause Mid-Flight* was released in 2010.

Elea Luis Manalo

...is third generation Filipino-American born and raised in the Bay Area and received her BA degree from the College of Notre Dame, Belmont, CA. She is married and currently resides in Daly City, CA. She has worked as an accountant but is now in the middle of changing careers and experimenting with her creative side. Elea loves spending time with family and friends, trying new things, traveling, and mostly being a new mom to her daughter, Jade Dylan.

Lisa Suguitan Melnick

...is a third generation Filipina-American whose daily life is a colorful melange of multi-cultural experience. She eats adobo with chopsticks, studies Afro-Cuban music, rescued a French dog. She—Lisa, not the dog—is a professor at the College of San Mateo teaching in both the Language Arts and Kinesiology divisions.

Veronica Montes

...lives in the San Francisco Bay Area with her husband and three daughters. Her short fiction has appeared in the literary journals *Bamboo Ridge*, *Prism International*, and *maganda*, as well as in the anthologies *Contemporary Fiction by Filipinos in America*, *Growing Up Filipino I & II*, *Going Home to a Landscape: Writings by Filipinas*, and *Philippine Speculative Fiction V*.

OSCAR PEÑARANDA
...His prose and poetry have been anthologized internationally. He is the author of award winning books, *Full Deck*, *Jokers Playing* and *Seasons By the Bay*. In 2012 he received the *Gawad ng Pambansang Alagad ni Balagtas* by the Unyon ng mga Manunulat ng Pilipinas for his lifetime achievements. He has been an educator for over 40 years and was a leader in the development of Bilingual Education in the San Francisco schools and the Filipino program at James Logan High School in Union City, California.

FELICIA PEREZ
...is a psychology instructor at Diablo Valley College and Ohlone College. She is of mixed heritage; Filipino from her paternal side and English/Scottish/German from her maternal side. For most of her life, she felt disconnected from her Filipino culture. Upon her father's death in 2005, she felt compelled to make a connection with her Filipino ancestral roots as part of her grieving process. As a result, she delved wholeheartedly into the history, culture and spiritual traditions on her journey to wholeness.

ROBERT V. RAGSAC, SR.
...is a retired space systems engineer. He worked in the aerospace industry in applied research, program management, and consulting positions. He is first generation American-born of Filipino parents who migrated to California in 1927 and is currently active in documenting the experiences of First Wave Filipinos in Santa Clara Valley during the 1930s-1940s.

MARIVIC REYES-RESTIVO
...left the Philippines when she was three months old and lived in various cities in Asia, Canada and the U.S., where her father, a diplomat, was assigned. Her visits to

the Philippines left a strong impression on her, providing inspiration for her stories.

Tony Robles
...is a fourth generation San Franciscan, poet, children's author and co-editor of *Poor Magazine*. Tony is a housing advocate in San Francisco working with seniors fighting displacement and gentrification. His forthcoming novel *Fillmore Flip* is based on the story of Filipinos living in the San Francisco Fillmore District. Tony is the nephew of Maniltown poet and historian, Al Robles.

Victoria Santos
...is a founding member of Filipinos for Affirmative Action (now Filipino Advocates for Justice) and was its first executive director. She is currently president of the FANHS-East Bay Chapter. In 2012, Vicky and her mother Constance, each received the 100 Most Influential Filipina Women in the U.S. award from the Filipina Women's Network. She expects to complete a memoir about her mother in the next year.

Adrian James Sobredo
...is a sophomore at the University of the Pacific (UOP) in Stockton, CA. He was a sophomore at Saint Mary's High School in Stockton when he presented an earlier version of this paper on Filipino Identity at the FANHS Conference at Seattle, in July 2010. He studied piano with Professor Frank Wiens of the Conservatory of Music at UOP for 7 years until he was 17. He also studied and practiced Filipino Martial Arts, Escrima, with Grandmaster Tony Somer and Master Joel Juanitas of Bahala Na Martial Arts. His parents, James and Lourdes Sobredo are lifetime FANHS members; his father is a founding member of Berkeley-East Bay FANHS Chapter.

Lourdes Sobredo
...is a grateful granddaughter of a Filipino farm worker who lived in America from 1929-1995. She is a retired California State Employment Development Administrator who holds a bachelor's degree in Psychology from UCLA and a master's in Public Administration from the University of San Francisco. She serves on the Parent Association Board for the University of the Pacific in Stockton, CA where her son,

Adrian, attends college. She is a member of the Executive Board of Global Majority, an international non-profit organization working towards making peace happen by non-violent conflict resolution through education and advocacy. She and her husband, James Sobredo, are lifetime members of the Filipino American Historical Society.

JANET STICKMON
...is a professor of Humanities and teaches Filipina(o)-American Heritage and Intro to African Studies at Napa Valley College. Stickmon is the author of *Crushing Soft Rubies—A Memoir* and *Midnight Peaches, Two O'clock Patience—A collection of Essays, Poems, and Short Stories on Womanhood and the Spirit*.

LEWIS SUZUKI
...was born in Los Angeles and currently lives in Berkeley. He studied in Japan, Los Angeles, New York, and Oakland and is known for his bold impressionistic use of color integrating western watercolor techniques with Japanese calligraphy to produce a strong, well-defined style. He is the recipient of numerous awards from various regional and national shows.

CLIFTON TRINIDAD
...is a second generation Filipino American, born and raised in San Francisco, CA. He received his undergraduate degrees from City College of San Francisco and San Francisco State University and advanced degrees from the University Oklahoma and the University of Nebraska. He served 22 years, seven months and one day in the United States Army and is retired from active service. Clifton continues to work for the Army as a civilian and lives in the Tidewater region of Virginia.

MONICA VALERIO
...was born and raised in the Bay Area and currently resides in Alameda, CA. She is seventh of twelve children. She has one daughter, Yvonne, who lives in Las Vegas. In her spare time she enjoys travelling and teaching Disaster Preparedness for the American Red Cross, Bay Area.

Jean Vengua
...is a writer and artist, and the author of poetry, *Prau*, and a chapbook, *The Aching Vicinities*. With Mark Young, she co-edited the *First Hay(na)ku Anthology*, and *The Hay(na)ku Anthology Vol. II*. Her poetry and essays have been published in many journals and anthologies.

Nikki Vilas
...was born and raised in Berkeley, CA. She is a semi-retired insurance professional who now spends her time focused on her passion for fabric art and music, family and friends.

Peter Kenichi Yamamoto
...is a 60-year-old mixed race Japanese American poet and community worker. He has had the intense pleasure of knowing and working with the great poet Al Robles. Pete spent the last three years of the International Hotel's existence living with the *Manongs* there, was evicted with them in August of 1977 and currently hangs out in Nihomachi, San Francisco.

Carlos Ziálcita
...was born in Manila and grew up in San Francisco, CA, after coming to the U.S. in 1958. He has been part of the San Francisco Bay Area jazz and blues scene for several decades as a harmonica player, singer, bandleader and educator. Ziálcita is the founder and producer of the San Francisco Filipino American Jazz Festival and the past Executive director of the Alameda Multicultural Community Center. He is one of the contributing writers to *Positively Filipino* magazine and *Images of America: Filipinos in San Francisco* (Arcadia Press, 2011).

Myrna Ziálcita
...is a long time activist, community organizer, and dreamer. She is a founder/director of the San Francisco Filipino American Jazz Festival along with a group of like-minded artists and activists. Myrna is passionate about family, artists, artists' rights, social justice for all people, and music.

Glossary

Adobo: marinated or pickled pork or chicken.

Anak: child, son, daughter

Asawa: spouse

Aswang: form of spirit (bird with long beak) that eats unborn babies

Babaylan: healer

Barangay: an administrative division within a town or city; barrio, district

Bagoong: fermented fish, shrimp, or other seafood

Balikbayan: an expatriate visiting the Philippines

Banana turon: wrapped deep fried banana

Blackapina: Black, Filipino-American Woman

Bunkhouse: sleeping quarters on a ranch or in a camp

Campo: farm labor camp

Carabao: water buffalo

Char siu bau: pork bun

Cebuano: language spoken in Cebu, Philippines

Daguhoy Lodge: Stockton, CA Chapter of the fraternal organization of the *Legionarios del Trabajo*

Debut: coming out party for teenage girl

Dios ti agngina: (Ilocano) Thank you

FANHS: Filipino American National Historical Society

Flip gig: event (dance) sponsored by Filipino groups/organizations

Hapa: Hawaiian term for racially mixed person

HSPA: Hawai'i Sugar Plant Association

I-Hotel: International Hotel located on Kearny Street, San Francisco's Chinatown district whose tenants, mainly Filipinos and Chinese, lived from 1930s until the hotel was bulldozed to make room for a parking lot

Ilocano (Ilokano): language spoken in Luzon, Northern Philippines

Kababayan: friends; town mates

Kabsat: Ilocano for brother / sister

Kadkadua: Ilocano word for placenta, twin, companion, to journey with spirit

Kalokohan: foolishness, craziness

Kulintang: musical instruments (gongs) from the southern region of the Philippines

Kuripot: stingy

Kuya: elder brother

Lechon: roast pork from a pig that is slow cooked; meat of pig cooked slowly in a pit

Little Manila: Filipino Town in Stockton, CA

Lolo: grandfather

Lola: grandmother

Lumpia: deep fried meat and/or veggies rolled in a wrapper

Manang: elder sister

Manong: elder brother

Musubi: sushi rice and spam wrapped in Nori seaweed

Nisei: second generation Japanese

Palenque: market

Pancit (pansit): noodle dish

Pinay: Filipina

Sala: living room

Sakadas: first group of Filipino sugar cane workers who arrived in Hawaii in 1906

Tagalog: national language spoken in the Philippines

Tinikling: Filipino dance using bamboo poles

TnT: Abbreviation of the Tagalog *tago ng tago* (constantly hiding) refering to the undocumented Filipino who decides to stay in the U.S.

Utang na loob: (Tagalog) literally "debt within," a deep sense of gratitude that one feels towards someone and that at some time needs to be paid back, reciprocated

Visayan: language spoken in the Visayan islands; person from the Visayan Islands

Waray: language spoken in the Visayan region